LECTURES
IN
AMERICA

LECTURES
IN
GERTRUDE STEIN
AMERICA

 VINTAGE BOOKS

A Division of Random House, New York

FIRST VINTAGE BOOKS EDITION, April 1975

Copyright, 1935, by The Modern Library, Inc.

Copyright renewed 1962 by Alice B. Toklas

All rights reserved under International and Pan-American Copyright Conventions. Published in the United States by Random House, Inc., New York. Distributed in Canada by Random House of Canada Limited, Toronto. Originally published by The Modern Library, Inc., in 1935.

Library of Congress Cataloging in Publication Data

Stein, Gertrude, 1874–1946.
  Lectures in America.
  Reprint of the ed. published by Modern Library, New York.
  CONTENTS: What is English literature.—Pictures.—Plays.—The gradual making of the making of Americans. [etc.]
  I. Title.
PS3537.T323L4 1975   814'.5'2   74–17454
ISBN 0–394–71477–6

Manufactured in the United States of America

TO BERNARD

WHO COMFORTINGLY AND ENCOURAGINGLY

WAS LISTENING

AS THESE WERE BEING WRITTEN

WHAT IS
ENGLISH
LITERATURE

ONE cannot come back too often to the question what is knowledge and to the answer knowledge is what one knows.

What is English literature that is to say what do I know about it, that is to say what is it. What is English literature, by English literature I mean American literature too.

Knowledge is the thing you know and how can you know more than you do know. But I do know a great deal about literature about English literature about American literature.

There is a great deal of literature but not so much but that one can know it. And that is the pleasant the delightful the fascinating the peaceful thing about literature that there is a great deal of it but that one can all one's life know all of it.

One can know all of it and one can know it all one's life and at any moment in one's life one can know all of it. There it is right in you right inside you right behind you. Perhaps in front of you but this you do not know. To be sure it has been more or less truly said about English literature that until about fifty years ago a first class English writer appeared almost every ten years, since that time it has been necessary to very much help if not to replace it by American literature. And so I say one can have at any one moment in one's life all of English literature inside you and behind you and what you do not yet know is if it is in front of you, you do not know if there is going to be any more of it. However very likely there is, there is at any rate going to be more American literature. Very likely.

At any rate it is a pleasure to know that there is so much English literature and that any any moment in one's life it is all inside you. At any rate it is all inside me. At any rate that is what I know. And now what is it that I do know about the English literature that is inside me, that is in me completely in me any moment of my living.

English literature has been with us a long time, quite a few hundreds of years, and during all that time it has had a great deal to do and also it has a great deal to not do.

This as a whole thing could be told in a couple of sentences but it is necessary to make it a great deal longer. Anybody, even I, can understand that necessity.

What has it had to do and what has it had not to do and how does one know one from the other, know what it has had to do from what it has had not to do.

In English literature there is a great deal of poetry and there is a great deal of prose and sometimes the poetry and the prose has had something to do one with the other and very often not. Besides this there has been again and again in English literature the question can one serve god and mammon, and the further question if one can should one. But the important question can remain and does remain what is god and mammon insofar as it concerns English literature. Has this question to do with prose and with poetry as both or as either one. I wish to very largely go into this because in it is the whole description of the whole of English literature and with it and after it although not entirely out of it comes American literature.

But to begin at any beginning at least as a beginning is.

There are two ways of thinking about literature as the history of English literature, the literature as it is a history of it and the literature as it is a history of you. Any one of us and anyway those of us that have always had the habit of reading have our own history of English literature inside us, the history as by reading we have come to know it. Then there is the history as the English people came to do it. Every one's own history of English literature is their own until they tell it to somebody else as I am now telling mine. The history of English literature as it was written is English Literature's History and that too most of any of us who have to read do know.

There is then also the English people's history of their English literature but then after all that is their affair as far as I am concerned, as I am deeply concerned, it is none of my business.

It is awfully important to know what is and what is not your business. I know that one of the most profoundly exciting moments of my life was when at about sixteen. I suddenly concluded that I would not make all knowledge my province.

And so my business is how English literature was made inside me and how English literature was made inside itself.

What does literature do and how does it do it. And what does English literature do and how does it do it. And what ways does it use to do what it does do.

If it describes what it sees how does it do it. If it describes what it knows how does it do it and what is the difference between what it sees and what it knows. And then too there is what it feels and then also there is what it hopes and wishes and then too there is what it would see if it could see and then there is what it explains. To do any or all of these things different things have to be done. Most of them are being done all the time by literature. And how has English literature done it.

As you come slowly to become acquainted with English Literature there are two things that at first do not interest you, explanations, that is one thing, and what it is that is felt, that is another thing. Most people all their later lives like these things the best in literature those of them who concern themselves with English literature by reading it.

They like explanations and they like to know how they felt, how they felt by the others feeling but anyway and principally how they felt.

The thing that has made the glory of English literature is description simple concentrated description not of what happened nor what is thought or what is dreamed but what exists and so makes the life the island life the daily island life. It is natural that an island life should be that. What could interest an island as much as the daily the completely daily island life. And in the descriptions the daily, the hourly descriptions of this island life as it exists and it does exist it does really exist English literature has gone on and on from Chaucer until now. It does not go on so well now for several reasons, in the first place they are not so interested in their island life because they are in short they are not so interested. And in the next place it is not as much an island life.

But in the beginning and then for an endless long going on there was there is the steady description of the daily life the daily island life. That makes a large one third of the glory of English literature.

Then there is the poetry that too comes out of a daily island life, because granted that a daily island life is what it is and the English daily island life has always been completely what it is, it is necessary that poetry is not what they lose or what they feel but is the things with which they are shut up, that is shut in, in the daily the simply daily island life. And so the poetry of England is so much what it is, it is the poetry of the things with which any of them are shut in in their daily, completely daily island life. It makes very beautiful poetry because anything shut in with

15

you can sing. There are the same things in other countries but they are not mentioned not mentioned in that simple intense certain way that makes English poetry what it is.

It is easy to know all that.

So that is something that has made several sides of English literature what it is.

And so to begin again to go on.

When anybody at any time comes to read English literature it is not at all necessary that they need to know that England is an island, what they need to know and that in reading any real piece of English literature they do know is that the thing written is completely contained within itself.

That is one of the reasons why in English literature there has been less question as to whether one should serve God and Mammon. There may inevitably be a question as to whether there is any god and mammon in respect to the inner existence of English literature. Because of there being really no vital question as to the God and Mammon and which is which in serving literature in English literature English literature has existed each piece of it inside itself in a perfectly extraordinary degree compared with other literatures that is other modern literatures and this gives it at once its complete solidity, its complete imagination, its complete existence.

When I was a child I was always completely fascinated by the sentence, he who runs may read. In

England running and reading is one because any one can read, and since any one can read does it make any difference how or why they run. Not on an island. In fact insofar as they run they are there there where they read just as much as not.

I am trying not to give to myself but to you a feeling of the way English literature feels inside me.

I have been thinking a great deal as to the question of serving God or mammon, and that in the case of most peoples, certainly peoples who live on continents it is not possible to do both not in making literature, but in English literature generally in English literature the question does not arise, because since the life of the island the daily life of the island goes on so completely and daily and entirely, there is no possibility, granting that it is all included and it always is, there is no possibility that in satisfying anybody there is not the satisfying everybody and so there is no question as between serving God and Mammon. There is enormously such a question for anybody living on a continent and the reason why I will go into largely as English literature connects with American literature. Not that it really does connect and yet not that it really does not. But this again is another matter.

To begin again then not begin again but just to state how English literature has come to be, came to be in me. In short what English literature is.

As I say description of the complete the entirely

complete daily island life has been England's glory. Think of Chaucer, think of Jane Austen, think of Anthony Trollope, and the life of the things shut up with that daily life is the poetry, think of all the lyrical poets, think what they say and what they have. They have shut in with them in their daily island life but completely shut in with them all the things that just in enumeration make poetry, and they can and do enumerate and they can and do make poetry, this enumeration. That is all one side of English literature and indeed anybody knows, where it grows, the daily life the complete daily life and the things shut in with that complete daily life.

The things being shut in are free and that makes more poetry so very much more poetry. It is very easy to understand that there has been so much poetry written in England.

On a continent even in small countries on a continent, the daily life is of course a daily life but it is not held in within as it is on an island and that makes an enormous difference, and I am quite certain that even if you do not see it as the same anybody does see that this if it is the truth is the truth. If it is the truth about English literature it is the truth about English literature.

It is a comparatively early thing to know English literature as English literature to those of us who read as naturally as we read that is as we run.

It begins if it begins it begins with Lamb's tales of

Shakespeare. And how are they the island daily life the English island daily life. But they are. And they are because of their poetry, and the poetry is because of the reality of all the life that is shut in, so completely sweetly, so delicately really shut in with their daily life.

I remember well I cannot say I do remember but I do feel and I did feel as if I did feel and did remember and do remember this.

And in the poetry of that time in their poetry is there any question of the difference in literature between its serving god and mammon.

Yes perhaps a little somewhat of that time. They knew their style knew that there were two styles. There was a style that those who run may read and there was a style too a style that those who read do not run. They need not run because there is nothing to run with or from.

That is the difference between serving god and serving mammon, and the period after the Chaucer time to the Pope Gibbon Johnson time was such a time. And how does one, how does one not run.

As I talk of serving god and mammon I do not of course mean religion in any sense excepting the need to complete that which is trying to fill itself up inside any one. And this may be part of the same inside in one or it may not. If it is then it is a complete daily life, if it is not then it is not.

As I say in that period from Chaucer to Pope

Gibbon and Johnson and Swift, a great many things filled up everybody that had to be filled, of course it is only those who have an active need to be completely completed who have all this as a bother.

As I say during this long period, the daily island life was there completely literally and daily and simply there, the poetry of the things shut in with that daily life were there but other things were there too and these other things were due to other origins and all these origins at that time were just sufficiently disturbing to make it possible for style to know that there is a serving god a serving mammon for those who write as they write. What else can they do.

During this long period and it was a long period, a very strongly long period a great many things happened in England and as they happened inside England they to a certain extent destroyed or at least confused the daily island life.

When the confusion comes to an island from the outside it is soon over and if not over then absorbed, that is what happened in the beginning of this period the norman conquest but when the confusion comes from the inside then it is a very confused confusion because it is a confusion inside the daily island life. This is what happened in all the latter part of this long period the English civil wars the period from Chaucer to Swift Gibbon Pope and Johnson and then again it settled down to being an island daily life only there were things left over from the late confusion and that was then the eighteenth century English literature and then there was the nineteenth century and then there was not any more a confusion but a complete settling in into the daily island life. What was outside was outside and what was inside was inside, and how could there be a question of god and mammon, when what is inside is inside and what is outside is outside there can be no confusing god and mammon.

Perhaps and perhaps not but that is at any rate one way in which living can be lived, literature can be made.

So the history of English literature is beginning to be clear, the history of English literature. Of course if the English people had not been what they were they would not have made out of the daily island life the literature they did make. That is true enough. Anything is true enough. But that certainly is.

The thing that happened before Chaucer, the Norman conquest coming as it did from the outside was one of those things which as I say do not produce confusion. They upset things for a while but they do not confuse things, a very different matter. And so when all that was over the thing English literature had still to do was to describe the daily island life and Chaucer did it, and the making of poetry of the things shut in with that daily island life and Chaucer certainly did it. Anybody that knows can certainly remember that. But and that must not be forgotten, words were in that daily island life which had not been there before and these words although they did not make for confusion did make for separation.

This separation is important in making literature, because there are so many ways for one to feel oneself and every new way helps, and a separating way may help a great deal, indeed it may, it may, it may help very much. And this did.

As you may or may not know I read a great deal of Elizabethan prose and poetry and in this period I felt the culmination of all of this. There was no confusion but there still was left over separation and this left over separation made a division in the writer of writing. He knew that there were two things to do and which of the things did he have to do. There was a choice at that time a choice as to how a writer should write. And this choice when there is a choice a writer can and does feel as a choice between serving god and mammon. This choice has nothing to do with religion, it has nothing to do with success. It has to do with something different than that, it has to do with completion.

How is anything completed. And if it is not might it, and is there a choice.

In the whole of the Elizabethan literature one feels this something.

There is no confusion but there is a separation and to any one doing it that is writing, I am speaking of the Elizabethans to themselves inside them, there was this bother.

And it was natural that there should be this bother. God and Mammon, god and mammon, it was left over and it was there and in all the Elizabethans it was there this bother, this choice, in every minute in their writing. There was the daily island life and it made poetry and it made prose but also there was this separation and it made poetry and it made prose but the choice the choice was the thing. In a true daily island life a choice is not the thing. It was the outside separation that had come to be an inside separation that made this thing. Think about it in any Elizabethan, any Elizabethan writing, in any Elizabethan who was writing.

And words had everything to do with it.

And now perhaps I had better explain a little more clearly what I mean by serving god and mammon in literature that is as a writer making literature.

When I say god and mammon concerning the writer writing, I mean that any one can use words to say something. And in using these words to say what he has to say he may use those words directly or indirectly. If he uses these words indirectly he says what he intends to have heard by somebody who is to hear and in so doing inevitably he has to serve mammon. Mammon may be a success, mammon may be an effort he is to produce, mammon may be a pleasure he has from hearing what he himself has done, mammon may be his way of explaining, mammon may be a laziness that needs nothing but going on, in short mammon may be anything that is done indirectly. Now serving god for a writer who is writing is writing anything directly, it makes no difference what it is but it must be direct, the relation between the thing done and the doer must be direct. In this way there is completion and the essence of the completed thing is completion. I have had a very great deal to say about this in the life of Henry James in my Four in America and I am not going to say any more about this now. But slowly you will see what I mean. If not why not.

But to return to English literature.

English literature when it is directly and completely describing the daily island life beginning with Chaucer and going on to now did have this complete quality of completeness. The lyric poets of England who described the things that are shut in with that daily island life also had this directness of completion.

But and this is very important during just before and the Elizabethan period there was another bother there was separation, separation between completion and incompletion and everybody dimly knew something of such a thing inside them.

If you like it was because the two languages were just coming to be one it was if you like because, although they were living the daily island life, they still, a considerable part of them, still had a memory of not having been living a daily island life. And this made a strange bother that any one can feel in the writing, the writing of any one writing during all that time. And that is a natural enough thing.

It is in all the prose and all the poetry of that long period. It all moves so much, and that is its most characteristic quality it all moves so much, it moves up and down and forward and back and right and left and around and around. And that is what makes it so exciting. And also what makes it inside itself so separating.

If you think in detail of the writing of any one writing in that long period you will know what I mean. Think of the one you know the best and you will see what I mean. There was no confusion, as I say the trouble had come from the outside and had been absorbed in the inside and in the process of absorption as there is in any healthy digestion there was no confusion but inevitably in concluding digestion there was separation.

And this is very much to be seen in the writing and there was very much writing, in that period. It was natural that there would be a great deal of writing because liveliness and choice inevitably produces a great deal of writing.

There was then at this period constant choice constant decision and the words have the liveliness of being constantly chosen.

That is what makes that the literature that it is.

And as there was all during that period the necessity of choice and the liveliness of choosing there was also all through that period the necessity of completing. Because why choose if there is not to be completion. And so they knew they quite knew the difference between being serving god and serving mammon, the difference between direct and indirect, the difference between separation and completion. They knew. And they knew it as they knew it. That too is a very real thing. And so although all through that period there was the daily island life, they were digesting there being that and it not always having been.

And that made for the writing that was being done then by everybody writing.

Then came the period after a period when they did not write so very much, because first it was all confused the disturbing of the daily island life having come from within, English Civil War, it was confused, and then we come to the beginning when everything was clear again and the daily island life was being lived with so much clarity that there could be nothing but the expression of that being that thing. That was the period that made Swift and Gibbon and Pope and Johnson and they had no longer to choose their words they could have all the pleasure in their use. And they did. No one ever enjoyed the use of what they had more than they did. There was no separation anywhere, the completeness was in the use.

As one says this one feels that.

As I say the pleasure of a literature is having it all inside you. It is the one thing that one can have all inside one.

This makes literature words whether you choose them whether you use them, whether they are there whether or not you use them and whether they are no longer there even when you are still going on using them. And in this way a century is a century. One century has words, another century chooses words, another century uses words and then another century using the words no longer has them.

All this as you have it inside you settles something it settles what you have when you write anything, it settles what you complete if you complete anything, it settles whether you address something as you express anything. In short it settles what you do as you proceed to write which you certainly do, that is which I certainly do.

As I say then each century has its way and by century of course one may mean a longer or shorter time but generally speaking a century is generally and almost always somewhere about a hundred years.

And so although and all through there was in England in English literature the complete and direct and simple and real description of their daily life, their daily life as they lived it every day on their island and which made their real solid body of writing and there was always too the description which made their lyric poetry the description of all the daily life of everything that was shut in inside their daily living, of all the things that grew and flew and were there to be in their daily living, in each century because of the outside coming to penetrate inside and then having become inside became inside, or because the inside caused confusion in the inside or because the decision of inside made all the inside as settled as if there never had been an outside or again later and this was in the nineteenth century when the inside had become so solidly inside that all the outside could be outside and still the inside was all inside, in each generation it effected writing because after all the way you write has everything to do with where you are insofar as you are anywhere, and of course and inevitably you are somewhere.

So once again all English literature being all inside you or inside me let me see how each century did as they were to see, that is as they were to say.

It is nice thinking how different each century is and the reason why. It is also nice to think about how differently the words sound one next to each other in each century and the reason why.

It is nice to feel the sound as the words next each other sound so differently.

I have always been very fond of the books that have little quotations at the head of each chapter. I like it particularly when the quotations are very varied and many of them of more or less important writers. I like it too sometimes when the quotations are only from one or two writers. It brings out with great clearness the way words sound next to each other even the same words when the century is different and the writer is different. I am very fond in that way of coming to feel how completely what is written comes to say what it does.

But to begin again as to what the different centuries do and how they do it and familiar as it is because it all is so familiar, it is all different. English literature then is very solid, and its reality is real and its poetry very poetry. And it did change in each century.

I am not very good at dates but there were generally speaking five centuries and now we are in the twentieth century which makes a sixth century and for this we go to America. And so to begin now. That is to begin again with any of them any of the five of them of English literature.

I wish I could make it as real to you the difference in which words phrases and then the gradual changes in each century were and as I realise them. I wish I could. I really wish I could. Because if I could well after that words and the way they say that for which they use them would make no difference or not any difference or all the difference.

You do remember Chaucer, even if you have not read him you do remember not how it looks but how it sounds, how simply it sounds as it sounds. That is as I say because the words were there. They had not yet to be chosen, they had only as yet to be there just there.

That makes a sound that gently sings that gently sounds but sounds as sounds It sounds as sounds of course as words but it sounds as sounds. It sounds as sounds that is to say as birds as well as words. And that is because the words are there, they are not chosen as words, they are already there. That is the way Chaucer sounds.

And then comes the long period. In that long period there were so many words that were chosen. Everybody was busy choosing words. In the poetry of that long period as well as in the prose everybody was livelily busy choosing words. And as the words were chosen, the sounds were very varied. And that is natural because each one liked what they liked. They did not care so much about what they said although they knew that what they said meant a great deal but they liked the words, and one word and another word next to the other word was always being chosen. Think well of the English literature of the sixteenth century and see how they chose the words, they chose them with so much choice that everything made the song they chose to sing. It was no longer just a song it was a song of words that were chosen to make a song that would sound like the words they were to sing. There is no use giving examples because it is true of everything that was written then. As they chose so early and often so late and often as they were everlastingly choosing and choosing was a lively occupation you have an infinite variety of length and shortness of words chosen of vowels and consonants of words chosen and and that is the important thing it was the specific word next to the specific word next it chosen to be next it that was the important thing. That made the glory that culminated in what is called Elizabethan. Just have it in your head and then go and look at it and you will have to see what I mean. There was no confusion then, things could be long that is words next to each other could be long and go on and very often they were short the words next to each other and they did go on but they were short, but each one was as it was chosen. There was no losing choosing in what they were saying. Never no never.

Confusion comes when they confuse what they are saying with the words they are choosing. And they knew. They knew, and a little one sees it coming even in the end of Shakespeare one sees it coming a little that there is confusion. This confusion comes when there is a giving up choosing, words next to each other are no longer so strictly chosen because there is intention to say what they are saying more importantly than completely choosing the words next each other which are to be chosen.

When that commences then there is confusion.

As I said at the end of the long period before the eighteenth century there was confusion, there was inside confusion. Something that had meant everything meant something but it no longer meant something in meaning everything and they all began to think what they wanted to say and how they wanted to say it.

The minute they all begin to think what they want to say and how they want to say it they no longer choose. And when they no longer choose then as far as writing goes they are no longer serving god they are serving mammon. No matter what it is or how fine it is or how religious it is the thing they want to say.

What is the use unless everybody knows what I want to say and what is the use if everybody does want to know everything that I want to say.

Well anyway at the end of the great epoch they began to think more of what they wanted to say as well as how they wanted to say it. Perhaps that should be turned around, they began to think more of how they wanted to say what they had come to decide to say than they did of choosing words to say what they chose the words to say the words next to each other to say.

That is pretty nearly what I do want to say.

And so we come to the confusion of which I spoke and which shows in Milton and lasted pretty well to Pope and Gibbon and Swift and Johnson.

Then as I say the confusion cleared. Nobody was any longer really interested in what anybody else was saying. They no longer chose the words to be one next to each other but they did choose and clearly chose all the words that were to go together.

By this time there was no confusion and no interest in what there was to say nor how they were to say it. There was no confusion. There was choosing but there was the choosing of a completed thing and so as there was no completing it as being chosen being in as much as it was there to choose being already a completed thing, they naturally had no separation inside in them, nothing was separated from anything. That made it all come as clearly as it came that made it all as completed as it was, that made it a whole thing chosen, and so the words were not next to each other but all the words as they followed each other were all together.

And that was all that.

If you think of the eighteenth century in English literature you will see how clear it was. But never forget that always it was an island life they lived and as they lived that daily island life they described daily that daily island life.

They wrote very much.

And now slowly there was coming something. The daily island life was still the daily island life, it would be more than ever that thing, because slowly a complete thing was nothing anybody was interested in choosing, because all they all lived as they only could live the daily island life and they came to own everything, and so although they brought nothing that they owned to be within the island life, as they owned everything outside and brought none of this inside they naturally were no longer interested in choosing complete things. That was the beginning of the nineteenth century.

Anybody can understand how natural this is.

If you live a daily island life and live it every day and own everything or enough to call it everything outside the island you are naturally not interested in completion, but you are naturally interested in telling about how you own everything. But naturally more completely are you interested in describing the daily island life, because more completely as you are describing the daily island life the more steadily and firmly are you owning everything you own which being practically everything could be called anything and everything.

Oh yes you do see.

You do see that.

And what has it to do with writing.

It has a great deal to do with writing.

And in this century in this nineteenth century anything could be a bother and was.

So now you see that up to the nineteenth century a number of things had been and gone and each time something had been and gone there had been a great deal of writing. That is again inevitable in a daily island life, if they write at all they write a great deal. Either nothing is worth writing about or everything is worth writing about. That anybody can understand.

And the daily life had always been worth writing about and so they always wrote a great deal. What else could they do. Granted that they lived this daily island life and realised it every day and were shut in every day with all of that daily island life every day what could they do but say it every day and as they said it every day they wrote it every day practically every day.

There had then as everybody knows been a great deal of English writing a great great deal of English writing, and it was poetry and it was prose.

The use of words whether the words were there as in Chaucer, whether they were livelily chosen to be next to each other one next to the other as in the long period after, and there were so many words chosen during that long period so many words chosen to be next to each other that there never can be a greater pleasure.

At the end of that long period when the words chosen to be next to each other gradually became troubled by the intention of how something was to be said rather than something that was something other than that something and how was the way that they had decided it should be said. That was the period of fashion and confusion the period of the restoration.

And then came the time after when everything was so complete that choosing or not choosing was not really any bother. They knew what to do because it was all so well done.

And then came the wars of Napoleon and England then came to own everything. And what happened.

As I say what happened was that the daily island life was more a daily life than ever. If it had not been it would have been lost in their owning everything and if it had been lost in their owning everything they would naturally have then ceased to own everything. Anybody can understand that.

They needed to be within completely within their daily island life in order to own everything outside as they were then really owning everything.

And what happened, what happened to their writing. Oh that is very interesting. It is interesting because it is very important about serving god and mammon, it is interesting because of what it did to words and phrases. It is interesting because we are still in the shadow of this thing. It is interesting.

In the first place did it change quickly.

And there is something you must always remember about wars that is about catastrophes, they make a change which is a change which is about to be a change go faster as much faster as a war can go, and even a slow war a slow catastrophe goes quite fast.

To be sure anything goes quite fast, that is changes quite fast. It is always an astonishment to me even in country family lives how much has changed how much a family life has changed, how completely a family life has changed say in five years.

This is always true but a catastrophe makes one say so more.

At any rate it was true although they did not in their daily life say that was true it was true in the life of English Literature.

After all it has not lasted so very long English literature and it has passed through so very much. And now came the nineteenth century and a great many things were gone.

That the words were there by themselves simply was gone. That the words were livelily chosen to be next one to the other was gone.

That the confusion of how and what was the way that any one at that time had to find was the way to say what they had to say was gone.

And the clarity of something having completion that too was gone completely gone.

And now what had they to do and how did they do it.

They were living their daily life and they owned everything, everything that existed anywhere outside.

And everybody wrote everybody always had written and how did they do it.

As I say we are still in the shadow of it.

One of the first things to notice is that the time now had come when they began to explain.

Before that in all the periods before things had been said been known been described been sung about, been fought about been destroyed been denied been imprisoned been lost but never been explained.

So then they began to explain. And we may say that they have been explaining ever since.

And as I say we are still in the shadow of it.

And what did they explain and why and what did it do to words and phrases.

And what did they do beside and what did living their island life inside and owning everything outside have to do with it.

There is explanation, the nineteenth century discovered explanation and what is the relation between explanation and sentimental emotion, such as the nineteenth century wrote. Is there any. Yes there is. There is a very distinct connection.

Of course I have read always read did nothing but read everything that was ever written in the nineteenth century. That is natural enough since I was born in the nineteenth century. What else could I do but read everything there was to read that was or had been written in the nineteenth century.

I had read almost read everything that was written in English in the eighteenth century, poetry prose and history, philosophy memoirs and novels, very long novels and I have read them all, I have read practically read and I was always reading, everything that was written in English in the eighteenth century. Of the long period that went before from Chaucer to the eighteenth century I read a good deal quite a good deal but of course not all, not all as I read what was written in the eighteenth century. In the nineteenth century I read more I read more than all and by that I mean that I read a great deal written in the nineteenth century that was just anybody's writing. And so it is easy to see that I having read so much that was written have a liking for reading writing. If not why not. But there is no if not, I do like reading writing. Now what did I slowly or not at all or very often or very well find out.

I have already told about some of the things I have found out and now to tell about what I more than found out what I knew every day as every day I read pretty nearly anything every day. And so to go on with explanation and how it came about and sentimental emotion and how it came about.

Some day I would like to be able to realise everything I feel about sentimental writing and what it is to each one who hears or writes or reads it. But first everything to tell everything about how differently the nineteenth century explained anything from the other times and what makes English nineteenth century literature what it is.

In the first place remember, I remember that words and then choice or not choice, knowing what there is to say or saying what they do say has been changing.

In the nineteenth century what they thought was

not what they said, but they said what they thought and they were thinking about what they thought.

This was different than the time that went before.

And now how do phrases come to be phrases and not sentences, that is the thing to know. Because in the nineteenth century it does. And that makes everything that makes the nineteenth century. And in order to understand, it must be understood that explaining was invented, naturally invented by those living a daily island life and owning everything else outside. They owned everything inside of course but that they had always done, but now they owned everything outside and that reinforced their owning everything inside, and that was as it was only more so but as they owned everything outside, outside and inside had to be told something about all this owning, otherwise they might not remember all this owning and so there was invented explaining and that made nineteenth century English literature what it is. And with explaining went emotional sentimental feeling because of course it had to be explained all the owning had to be told about its being owned about its owning and anybody can see that if island daily life were to continue its daily existing there must be emotional sentimental feeling.

To like to tell it like that again, and to remember all the books that were written and read, read by any one read by me, oh yes read, and still read.

As I say in the nineteenth century what they

thought was not what they said, but and this may sound like the same thing only it is not, they said what they thought and they were thinking about what they thought. This made the nineteenth century what it was.

If you live a daily life and it is all yours, and you come to own everything outside your daily life beside and it is all yours, you naturally begin to explain. You naturally continue describing your daily life which is all yours, and you naturally begin to explain how you own everything beside. You naturally begin to explain that to yourself and you also naturally begin to explain it to those living your daily life who own it with you, everything outside, and you naturally explain it in a kind of a way to some of those whom you own. All this leads you to that what you think is not what you say but you say what you think and you are thinking about what you think. Do you understand, if not it is perhaps because after all you have not read all English nineteenth century literature, but perhaps you have and if you have then you do understand. You must also then understand what explaining is and how it came to be.

Perhaps we are still under its shadow a little bit.

I am thinking of all the nineteenth century English literature that I have always read. There is so much of it and I have read so much of it and I have read it so often and I have so read it over and over again. And I am still reading it. I read it in long pieces and little pieces, it is a natural thing to do because after all when one picks up a book to read and if you read a great deal as I read a great deal books every day and many books every week of course inevitably I read many books I have read, and as I have read everything written in the nineteenth century, important unimportant, prose, poetry, history, science and some essays why naturally I read it again. What else can I do.

And so I know what it is.

That is natural enough.

What is it.

I have already said what it is and I think that is what it is. And in its being that, it is necessary that it was written in the way it was.

As I said the eighteenth century was clear and so there was a choice and the choice was a completed thing and what is a completed thing. A sentence is a completed thing and so the eighteenth century chose the completed sentence as a completed thing. Now what did the nineteenth century do.

As I explained it did not choose a completed thing. Anybody can understand that if you explain and the thing to be explained is that you leading your daily inside life own everything outside, it is not possible to choose a completed sentence a completed thing. That manifestly is not possible because if you have to explain the inside to the inside and the owning of the outside to the inside that has to be explained to the inside life and and the owning of the outside has to be explained to the outside it absolutely is not possible that it is to be done in completed sentences. Anybody can see that, anybody can. And so then how did the nineteenth century write.

They did not write in words that were simply words as Chaucer did. That would not help explain anything, it was too simple a thing to need or to be employed to make explaining. They did not choose words to be next to each other and to be lively just in being that in being next to each other because anything as lively as that could not own everything. Anybody can understand that. And as I have already said they could not content themselves with a completed thing that is choosing a whole sentence, because if a thing is a completed thing then it does not need explanation.

So what did they do and gradually if you think how from the eighteenth century to the nineteenth century the language gradually changed you will see that it proceeded to live by phrases, words no longer lived, sentences and paragraphs were divisions because they always are but they did not mean particularly much, but phrases became the thing. Think of the English writing in the height of the nineteenth century and you will see that it is so.

They thought about what they were thinking and if you think about what you are thinking you are bound to think about it in phrases, because if you think about what you are thinking you are not thinking about a whole thing. If you are explaining, the same thing is true, you cannot explain a whole thing because if it is a whole thing it does not need explaining, it merely needs stating. And then the emotional sentiment that any one living their daily living and owning everything outside needs to express is again something that can only be expressed by phrases, neither by words nor by sentences. Anybody ought to be able to realise this thing.

I do really definitely know that although some may think there are some exceptions there were really not except in the beginning when the eighteenth century was still lingering or toward the end when the twentieth century was beginning. There were really no exceptions.

Think really think about any big piece or any little piece of nineteenth century writing and you will see that it is true that it exists by its phrases. Its poetry does as well as its prose. Compare Jane Austen with Anthony Trollope and you will see what I mean and how the volume of the phrasing gradually grew and when you read Dickens, compare it with and they are both sentimental with Clarissa Harlowe and you will see what I mean. One lives by its whole the eighteenth century thing and the nineteenth century thing lives by its parts. You can see what I mean that this connects itself with explaining. The same thing is true with nineteenth century poetry. The lake poets had other ideas, they felt that it was wrong to live by parts

of a whole and they tried and they tried they wanted
to serve god not mammon, but they too inevitably as
they wrote longer and longer live by parts of the
whole, because after all mammon and god were inter-
changeable since in the nineteenth century England
lived its daily island life and owned everything outside. Oh yes you do see this. And so it goes on and on
and think of Tennyson. There you completely see
what I mean. And now we come to a new thing. I hope
you thoroughly understand that the nineteenth century wrote by its phrases and it wrote a great great
great deal and I have read it all and so have a good
many others. It is a soothing thing to rest upon, it is
more soothing than other things in spite of the fact
that a great many people who wrote it did not like it
as they knew they wrote. But it is a soothing thing to
write phrases, the sentiment of phrases is a soothing
thing and so we all of us always like reading nineteenth century writing, those of us who like to feel
soothed by something that touches feeling.

Do you feel the nineteenth century writing as it is.
I hope so. I do.

And toward the end of the nineteenth century there
was bound to be a change because after all nothing
goes on longer than it can.

And this quite naturally could not go on any longer
than it could any more than anything else did. And
this is where it connects on with American literature.

American literature all the nineteenth century

went on by itself and although it might seem to have been doing the same thing as English literature it really was not and it really was not for an excellent reason it was not leading a daily island life. Not at all nothing could be more completely not a daily island life than the life the daily life of any American. It was so completely not a daily island life that one may well say that it was not a daily life at all.

That is fundamental that is what the American writing inevitably is, it is not a daily life at all.

But before going on with this at all I am going on with English literature and although nothing much happened in the way of changes something did happen and this does help to connect with American writing.

As the time went on to the end of the nineteenth century and Victoria was over and the Boer war it began to be a little different in England. The daily island life was less daily and the owning everything outside was less owning, and, and this should be remembered, there were a great many writing but the writing was not so good. I remember very well, I was quite young then being very worried about England because there had been, one might quite say Kipling was the last one no really first class writing. The other writing of that period was the second class writing of the last generation, the young generation were doing the second class writing of the past generation,

Wells, Galsworthy, Bennett etc. And since then it has not changed.

But before this happened there was something else that connected itself with what was to be American, American writing, one might say Meredith, Swinburne etc. and this had to do with the fact that the daily living was ceasing to be quite so daily and besides that they were beginning not to know everything about owning everything that was existing outside of them outside of their daily living. And this had to do with phrasing.

Slowly the phrasing, you see it in Browning you see it in Swinburne and in Meredith and its culmination was in Henry James who being American knew what he was doing, it is to be seen that even phrases were no longer necessary to make emotion emotion to make explaining explaining.

As I say as daily living was no longer being so positively lived every day and they were not all of them so certainly owning everything outside them, explaining and expressing their feeling was not any longer an inevitable thing and so the phrase no longer sufficiently held what a phrase had to hold and they no longer said what they thought and they were beginning not to think about what they thought.

This brought about something that made neither words exist for themselves, nor sentences, nor choosing, it created the need of paragraphing, and the whole paragraph having been being made the whole paragraph had rising from it off of it its meaning.

If you think of the writers I have mentioned you will see what I mean.

As I say Henry James being an American knew best what he was doing when he did this thing.

Do you quite clearly see that now there has commenced really commenced paragraphing.

I once said in How to Write a book I wrote about Sentences and Paragraphs, that paragraphs were emotional and sentences were not. Paragraphs are emotional not because they express an emotion but because they register or limit an emotion. Compare paragraphs with sentences any paragraph or any sentence and you will see what I mean.

Paragraphs then having in them the quality of registering as well as limiting an emotion were the natural expression of the end of the nineteenth century of English literature. The daily island life was not sufficient any more as limiting the daily life of the English, and the owning everything outside was no longer actual or certain and so it was necessary that these things should be replaced by something and they were replaced by the paragraph. Do you quite see what I mean. I know quite completely what I mean. Think of Browning Meredith and Henry James and Swinburne and you will see what I mean. The phrases the emotion of phrases, the explaining in phrases that made the whole nineteenth century adequately felt and seen no longer sufficed to satisfy

what anybody could mean. And so they needed a paragraph. A phrase no longer soothed, suggested or convinced, they needed a whole paragraph. And so slowly
the paragraph came to be the thing, neither the words
of the earlier period, the sentence of the eighteenth
century, the phrases of the nineteenth century, but
the paragraphs of the twentieth century, and, it is
true, the English have not gone on with this thing
but we have we in American literature. In English
literature they just went back to the nineteenth century and made it a little weaker, and that was because
well because they were a little weaker. What else can
I say.

And so we come to American literature and why
they went on and we are the twentieth century
literature.

I will not tell a great deal about what I will tell just
a little about that.

I said I certainly have said that daily life was not
the daily life in America. If you think of the difference
between England and America you will understand it.

In England the daily island life was the daily life
and it was solidly that daily life and they generally
always simply relied on it. They relied on it so completely that they did not describe it they just had it
and told it. Just like that. And then they had poetry,
because everything was shut in there with them and
these things birds beasts woods flowers, roses, vio-
lets and fishes were all there and as they were all

there just telling that they were all there made poetry for any one. And there was a great deal of poetry there. That was English literature and it has lasted for some five hundred years or more and there is a great deal of it. All this now has been everything.

In America as I was saying the daily everything was not the daily living and generally speaking there is not a daily everything. They do not live every day. And as they do not live every day they do not have the daily living and so they do not have this as something that they are telling.

To be sure a number of them who have learned to write by reading and naturally they have learned to write by reading what English literature has been telling, a number of them tried to turn it into a telling of daily living daily American living but these even these although they did it as much as they could did not really succeed in doing it because it is not an American thing, to tell a daily living, as in America there is not any really not any daily daily living. So of course it is not to be told.

And now think how American literature tells something. It tells something because that anything is not connected with what would be daily living if they had it.

This is quite definitely not the same not the same as in English writing.

It has often been known that American literature in a kind of a way is more connected with English

Elizabethan than with later and that if you remember was at a time when words were chosen to be next one to the other and because in a kind of a way at that time it was a bother to feel inside one that one was a writer because things were separated away one thing from another thing, one way of choosing anything from another way of choosing.

Now all this is sufficiently different from what is American but still it has something to do with it.

What there is to say is this.

Think about all persistent American writing. There is inside it as separation, a separation from what is chosen to what is that from which it has been chosen.

Think of them, from Washington Irving, Emerson, Hawthorne, Walt Whitman, Henry James. They knew that there is a separation a quite separation between what is chosen and from what there is the choosing. You do see that.

This makes what American literature is, something that in its way is quite alone. As it has to be, because in its choosing it has to be, that it has not to be, it has to be without any connection with that from which it is choosing.

Now you can see how different this is from English writing, which almost completely makes that from which it is chosen, indeed it makes it so completely that there is no choice there does not have to be any choosing.

You do see what I say.

And so, and this is the thing to know, American literature was ready to go on, because where English literature had ceased to be because it had no further to go, American literature had always had it as the way to go.

You understand that I tell you so. And it is so, as you can easily see, if you see what American literature always really has been and has had to be.

To go back to where Henry James, and Browning, and Swinburne and Meredith had come.

I told you they had come where they needed a whole paragraph to give off something that did come. And this they all did.

The others all stayed where they were, it was where they had come but Henry James knew he was on his way. That is because this did connect with the American way. And so although they did in a way the same thing, his had a future feeling and theirs an ending. It is very interesting.

And now do you see what I mean.

English literature than had a need to be what it had become. Browning Swinburne Meredith were no longer able to go on, they had come where they had come, because although island daily living was still island daily living every one could know that this was not what it was to be and if it was not to be this with all the outside belonging to it what was it to be. They Swinburne Browning and Meredith were giving the last extension, they were needing a whole paragraph to make it something that they could mention and in doing so the paragraph no longer said what all English literature had always said that alive or dead the daily life the daily island life was always led.

This is where they were.

And so as I say since everything one cannot say had gone away, but was no longer there to stay, it was necessary to have a whole paragraph to hold anything there at all. And so that ended that.

In the meantime Henry James went on. He too needed the whole paragraph because he too was just there, but, and that is the thing to notice, his whole paragraph was detached what it said from what it did, what it was from what it held, and over it all something floated not floated away but just floated, floated up there. You can see how that was not true of Swinburne and Browning and Meredith but that it was true of Henry James.

And so this makes it that Henry James just went on doing what American literature had always done, the form was always the form of the contemporary English one, but the disembodied way of disconnecting something from anything and anything from something was the American one. The way it had of often all never having any daily living was an American one.

Some say that it is repression but no it is not repression it is a lack of connection, of there being no connection with living and daily living because there is none, that makes American writing what it always has been and what it will continue to become.

And so there we are.

And now, the paragraph having been completely become, it was a moment when I came and I had to do more with the paragraph than ever had been done. So I thought I did. And then I went on to what was the American thing the disconnection and I kept breaking the paragraph down, and everything down to commence again with not connecting with the daily anything and yet to really choose something. But this is another story and I have told enough.

And now about serving god and mammon. The writer is to serve god or mammon by writing the way it has been written or by writing the way it is being written that is to say the way the writing is writing. That is for writing the difference between serving god and mammon. If you write the way it has already been written the way writing has already been written then you are serving mammon, because you are living by something some one has already been earning or has earned. If you write as you are to be writing then you are serving as a writer god because you are not earning anything. If anything is to be earned you will not know what earning is therefore you are serving god. But really there is no choice. Nobody chooses. What you do you do even if you do not yield to a temptation. After all a temptation is not very tempting. So anyway you will earn nothing. And so this is the history of English literature of all the writing written in English as I understand it.

PICTURES

IT is natural that I should tell about pictures, that is, about paintings. Everybody must like something and I like seeing painted pictures. Once the Little Review had a questionnaire, it was for their farewell number, and they asked everybody whose work they had printed to answer a number of questions. One of the questions was, what do you feel about modern art. I answered, I like to look at it. That was my real answer because I do, I do like to look at it, that is at the picture part of modern art. The other parts of it interest me much less.

As I say everybody has to like something, some people like to eat some people like to drink, some people like to make money some like to spend money, some like the theatre, some even like sculpture, some like gardening, some like dogs, some like cats, some people like to look at things, some people like to look at everything. Any way some one is almost sure to really like something outside of their real occupation. I have not mentioned games indoor and out, and birds and crime and politics and photography, but anybody can go on, and I, personally, I like all these things well enough but they do not hold my attention long enough. The only thing, funnily enough, that I never get tired of doing is looking at pictures. There is no reason for it but for some reason, anything reproduced by paint, preferably, I may even say certainly, by oil paints on a flat surface holds my attention. I do not really care for water colors or pastels, they do not really hold my attention.

I cannot remember when I was not so.

I like sign paintings and I do regret that they no longer paint the signs on the walls with oil paints. Paper with the things reproduced plastered on the wall does not do the same thing to me, it does not hold my attention. Neither does wall paper although wall paper does sometimes give the illusion of paint. But it does not do so enough, no not enough. I like to look at anything painted in oil on a flat surface although for nothing in the world would I want to be a painter or paint anything.

I have often wondered why I like the representation or the presentation of anything in oil on a flat surface but I have never been able to find out the reason why. It is simply a fact. I even like a curtain or a sign painted as they often do in Europe painted in oil of the things to be sold inside and I like a false window or a vista painted on a house as they do so much in Italy. In short anything painted in oil anywhere on a flat surface holds my attention and I can always look at it and slowly yes slowly I will tell you all about it.

When I look at landscape or people or flowers they do not look to me like pictures, no not at all. On the other hand pictures for me do not have to look like flowers or people or landscapes or houses or anything else. They can, they often do, but they do not have to.

Once an oil painting is painted, painted on a flat surface, painted by anybody who likes or is hired or is interested to paint it, or who has or has not been taught to paint it, I can always look at it and it always holds my attention. The painting may be good it may be bad, medium or very bad or very good but any way I like to look at it. And now, why does the representation of things that being painted do not look at all like the things look to me from which they are painted why does such a representation give me pleasure and hold my attention. Ah yes, well this I do not know and I do not know whether I ever will know, this. However it is true and I repeat that to give me this interest the painting must be an oil painting and any oil painting whether it is intended to look like something and looks like it or whether it is intended to look like something and does not look like it it really makes no difference, the fact remains that for me it has achieved an existence in and for itself, it exists on as being an oil painting on a flat surface and it has its own life and like it or not there it is and I can look at it and it does hold my attention.

That the oil painting once it is made has its own existence this is a thing that can of course be said of anything. Anything once it is made has its own existence and it is because of that that anything holds somebody's attention. The question always is about that anything, how much vitality has it and do you happen to like to look at it.

By anything here I really mean anything. Anything that happens anything that exists anything that is made has of course its own vitality and presumably some one or if not yet then there could presumably be sometime someone who would like to look at it. But does it really, that is is it true of everything does everything that is anything does it hold somebody's attention. Yes perhaps so. One certainly may say so. And so it comes back to the fact that anything having its own existence how much vitality has it and do you happen to like to look at it and does it hold your attention.

Now most of us live in ourselves that is to say in one thing and we have to have a relief from the intensity of that thing and so we like to look at something. Presidents of the United States of America are supposed to like to look at baseball games. I can understand that, I did too once, but ultimately it did not hold my attention. Pictures made in oil on a flat surface do, they do hold my attention, and so to go further into this matter.

The first thing I ever saw painted and that I remember and remembered seeing and feeling as painted, no one of you could know what that was, it was a very large oil painting. It was the panorama of the battle of Waterloo. I must have been about eight years old and it was very exciting, it was exciting seeing the panorama of the battle of Waterloo. There was a man there who told all about the battle, I knew a good deal about it already because I always read historical novels and history and I knew about the sunken road where the french cavalry were caught but though all that was exciting the thing that was exciting me was the oil painting. It was an oil painting a continuous oil painting, one was surrounded by an oil painting and I who lived continuously out of doors and felt air and sunshine and things to see felt that this was all different and very exciting. There it all was the things to see but there was no air it just was an oil painting. I remember standing on the little platform in the center and almost consciously knowing that there was no air. There was no air, there was no feeling of air, it just was an oil painting and it had a life of its own and it was a scene as an oil painting sees it and it was a real thing which looked like something I had seen but it had nothing to do with that something that I knew because the feeling was not at all that not at all the feeling which I had when I saw anything that was really what the oil painting showed. It the oil painting showed it as an oil painting. That is what an oil painting is.

Later when I was about eighteen I saw the actual battle field of the Battle of Gettysburg and the difference in emotion in seeing the actual battle field of the battle of Gettysburg and the panorama of the Battle of Waterloo is a thing that I very well remember. I knew of course I knew all about the battle of Gettysburg. When we were there it was a wonderful early summer day, and it was an entirely different thing from an oil painting. There were so many things back present and future, and a feeling of enjoying oneself and there it was and the whole thing was very complicated. I know what the battle field of the Battle of Gettysburg looks like in general and in detail and I know what I felt and I know what was said by us and what we said and the states that were represented but I do not know exactly what it looked like as I know exactly what the battle of Waterloo looked like at the Panorama of the battle of Waterloo which was an enormous circular oil painting. Do you begin to see a little bit what it is to be an oil painting. I have always liked looking at pictures of battle scenes but as I say I always like looking at pictures and then once after the war I saw the battle field of the battle of Metz. For a moment as I looked at it, it was a grey day and we were on our way back from Alsace to Paris and we had seen so many battle fields of this war and this one was so historical, it almost it did almost look like an oil painting. As I say things do not generally look to me like an oil painting. And just then into this thing which was so historical that it almost did look like an oil painting a very old couple of people a man and woman got out of an automobile and went to look at a grave at the way-side and the moment of its existence as an oil painting ceased, it became a historical illustration for a simple historical story. In connection with the Panorama of the Battle of Waterloo there was a description of the battle of Waterloo as told by Victor Hugo. If it had not rained on the twenty-sixth of March 1814 the fate of Europe would have been changed. I never really believed this because of course I had read so many English novels and so much English history about the battle of Waterloo but it was a perfectly definite picture of the battle of Waterloo and it had nothing whatever to do with an oil painting. It was the complete other thing of an oil painting. And now to go on with what an oil painting is.

The next thing I remember about an oil painting were the advent, in San Francisco I was still a child, of two very different paintings. One was by a man I think named Rosenthal who had been sent to Europe to develop his talent and he came back with a very large painting of a scene from Scott's Marmion the nun being entombed in a wall as a punishment. The other painting was Millet's Man with a Hoe. Both the pictures interested me equally, but I did not want a photograph of the Rosenthal picture but I did of the Man with a Hoe. I remember looking at it a great deal. And then we that is my brother and myself very moved not knowing exactly why but very moved showed the photograph to my eldest brother and he looked at it equally solemnly and then he said very decidedly, it is a hell of a hoe, and he was right.

But I still know exactly how the picture of the Man with a Hoe looked. I know exactly how it looked although having now lived a great deal in the french country I see the farmers constantly hoeing with just that kind of a hoe. The hoeing with just that kind of a hoe as I see them all the time and meet them all the time have nothing to do with Millet's Man with a Hoe but that is natural because I know the men as men, the hoe as a hoe and the fields as fields. But I still do know Millet's Man with a Hoe, because it was an oil painting. And my brother said it was a hell of hoe but what it was was an oil painting. Millet's pictures did have something that made one say these things. I remember not so many years ago at Bourg going through the monastery next to the cathedral of Brou. There unexpectedly in a little room was a cow, almost a real cow and it was an oil painting by Millet, and it did not startle me but there it was it was almost a cow but it was an oil painting and though I had not thought of a Millet for years, I did like it.

After this experience with Millet's Man with a Hoe and the Rosenthal picture I began to become educated aesthetically, first etchings, they were in those days reproduced in magazines and we used to cut them out and then we began to collect real etchings, not many but still a few, all this was still in San Francisco, Seymour Hayden, Whistler, Zorn and finally Meryon, but these two were much later, and Japanese prints. I took on all this earnestly but inevitably as they were not oil paintings they did not hold my attention. I do remember, still in San Francisco, a sign painting of a man painting a sign a huge sign painting and this did hold my attention. I used to go and look at it and stand and watch it and then it bothered me because it almost did look like a man painting a sign and one wants, one likes to be deceived but not for too long. That is a thing to remember about an oil painting. It bothered me many years later when I first looked at the Velasquez's in Madrid. They almost looked really like people and if they kept on doing so might it not bother one as wax works bother one. And if it did bother one was it an oil painting, because an oil painting is something that looking at it it looks as it is, an oil painting.

All this has to be remembered but to go back again.

The next thing that interested me in the way of an oil painting, still in San Francisco, were some paintings by a frenchman named Cazin. Of course perhaps none of you have ever heard of him.

He was one of the then new school of painters who being accepted officially in the salons were the commonplace end of the then still outlawed school of impressionists. Cazin made a field of wheat look almost like a field of wheat blowing in the wind. It did look like a field of wheat blowing in the wind and I was very fond of looking at fields of wheat blowing in the wind. In a little while I found myself getting a little mixed as to which looked most like a field of wheat blowing in the wind the picture of the field of wheat or the real field of wheat. When that happens one naturally gets discouraged. I may say one finally gets discouraged. One is not discouraged at first, one is confirmed in one's feeling about a field of wheat blowing in the wind and then gradually one is less pleased and at last one is discouraged. One does not like to be mixed in one's mind as to which looks most like something at which one is looking the thing or the painting. And so I rather lost interest in both.

There was another painting also by Cazin called Juan and Juanita or at least that is what I called it to myself because at that time I was reading a story that had these two names, I think actually it was called something biblical. Anyway it was a picture of two children lost in the desert and the desert was like the California deserts I knew. The desert this painted desert looked very like the desert but the children did not look really very much like children and so finally I preferred that picture to the field of wheat. I suppose I concluded that since the children did not really look as children looked to me probably neither did the blowing wheat nor the desert. All this of course was very dim inside me.

The next thing that impressed me in the way of oil painting was in Baltimore at the Walters Art Gallery the pictures of the Barbizon school, not Millet any longer but Daubignys and Rousseaus. Here once more the blue sky behind the rocks was the blue sky I knew behind rocks, and particularly the Rousseaus solidi-

fying for me the blue sky behind rocks held me. As
the pictures were small and the blue sky was small
the question of the real sky did not bother me, and
beside although it pleased me and I liked it it did not
really excite me. Then I went to Boston and there I
saw the first big Corots. The one in the Boston Museum the evening star. There again I felt peaceful
about it being a sky because after all it was filled with
association, it was not a thing in itself. It looked like
the evening star it looked as Tannhauser felt and
more than that one could feel how it looked and so
there was no bother. Later on, Corots always pleased
me but that I think was largely because they were so
gentle. I never was much troubled by anything in
connection with them.

Then I bought myself my first oil painting. It was
painted by an American painter called Shilling and
I wanted it because it looked like any piece of American country and the sky was high and there was a
cloud and it looked like something in movement and I
remember very well what it was like, and then again
it bothered me because after all which did I like most
the thing seen or the thing painted and what was a
thing in movement. I began to be almost consciously
bothered.

Then I went to Europe first Antwerp then Italy
then France then Spain and then later again France.
Of course all this in successive years, I naturally
looked at a great many pictures.

In Antwerp I only remember the colour of the Rubens' and that they were religious. I liked their colour. I liked pretty well liked their religion.

Then we went through France to Italy.

The Louvre at first was only gold frames to me gold frames which were rather glorious, and looking out of the window of the Louvre with the gold frames being all gold behind within was very glorious. I always like, as well as liked looking out of windows in museums. It is more complete, looking out of windows in museums, than looking out of windows anywhere else.

Then we went to Italy and my brother and I spent a long hot summer in Italy, in Florence and in Venice and in Perugia and I began to sleep and dream in front of oil paintings.

I did look out of the windows of the museums but it was really not necessary.

There were very few people in the galleries in Italy in the summers in those days and there were long benches and they were red and they were comfortable at least they were to me and the guardians were indifferent or amiable and I could really lie down and sleep in front of the pictures. You can see that it was not necessary to look out of the windows.

In sleeping and waking in front particularly of the Tintorettos the Giottos and the Castagnas, the Botticellis were less suited to that activity, they little as one can think it they bothered me because the

Italian flowers were just like the flowers in the Botti-celli pictures. I used to walk in the country and then I concluded that the Botticellis being really so like the flowers in the country they were not the pictures before which one could sleep, they were to my feel-ing, being that they looked so like the flowers in the country, they were artificial. You know what I mean artificial flowers. And I literally mean just that. At least that is the way I felt then about it. I liked Man-tegna then because he made me realize that white is a colour, and in a way he made me feel something about what oil paintings were that prepared me for much that was to come later.

As I say in sleeping and waking in front of all these pictures I really began to realize that an oil painting is an oil painting. I was beginning after that to be able to look with pleasure at any oil painting.

I had another curious experience concerning oil painting at about that same time.

I went into Italian churches a great deal then and I began to be very much interested in black and white marble. Even other colored marbles. I went in Rome to Saint John without the walls and I did not like the marble and then I looked at the marble I did like and I began to touch it and I found gradually that if I liked it there was always as much imitation oil painted marble as real marble. And all being mixed together I liked it. It was very hard to tell the real from the false. I spent hours in those hot summer days feeling marble to see which was real and which was not. I found that granite pillars if they were four were some of them make believe if they gave me pleasure, some could be real but some had to be painted, of course they did, if it was all marble or if it was all granite there was nothing to content the eye by deceiving it. Of course anybody could come to know that.

And so I began to look at all and any oil painting. I looked at funny pictures in churches where they described in a picture what had happened to them, the ex-voto pictures. I remember one of a woman falling out of a high two wheeled cart, this a picture of what happened to her and how she was not killed. I looked at all oil paintings that I happened to see and not consciously but slowly I began to feel that it made no difference what an oil painting painted it always did and should look like an oil painting.

And so one comes to any oil painting through any other oil painting.

Then we went to Spain and there I looked and looked at pictures. I do not think there were any windows to look out of in the Prado museum in those days. Any way I only remember looking and looking at pictures. The gallery was not arranged in those days and you found your pictures. It was my first real experience in finding pictures. I then for the first time really began to think about them. I liked Rubens landscapes because they all moved together, people landscape animals and color. I liked Titians because they did not move at all and as they did not move they were noble. The Velasquez bothered me as I say because like the Cazins of my youth they were too real and yet they were not real enough to be real and not unreal enough to be unreal.

And then I found Greco and that really excited me.

There the oil painting was pure it neither moved nor was still nor was it real. I finally came to like them best. I liked them because every thing in them was so long and I liked them because they were so white. I have never forgotten what white is since.

Then I came back to France and there at once I forgot Greco because there was the Louvre and somehow there with the gold frames and all, there was an elegance about it all, that did not please me, but that I could not refuse, and in a way it destroyed oil paintings for me.

I completely for a while forgot about oil paintings.

I did not care at that time for elegance and since oil painting, so the Louvre had decided for me, were fundamentally elegant I lost interest in oil paintings. I did not get back any interest in them until the next year.

To finish a thing, that is to keep on finishing a thing, that is to be one going on finishing so that something is a thing that any one can see is a finished thing is something. To finish a thing so that any one can know that that thing is a finished thing is something.

To make a pretty thing so that any one can feel that the thing is a pretty thing is something.

To begin a thing that any one can see is begun is something. To begin a pretty thing so that any one can see that a pretty thing has been begun is something.

PORTRAITS AND PRAYERS—PAGE 54—RANDOM HOUSE.

I remember much later than that being very bothered by Courbet. I had commenced looking at later oil paintings, that is later than old museum pictures. I liked David then because he was so dry and Ary Sheffer because he was so tender and Greuze because he was so pretty and they all painted people to look like people that is more or less to look like people, to look like people more or less, and it did not make any difference.

But Courbet bothered me. He did really use the color that nature looked like that any landscape looked like when it was just like itself as you saw it in passing. Courbet really did use the colors that nature looked like to anybody, that a water-fall in the woods looked like to anybody.

And what had that to do with anything, in fact did it not destroy a little of the reality of the oil painting. The paintings of Courbet were very real as oil paintings, they existed very really as oil painting,

74

but did the colors that were the colors anybody could see trees and water-falls naturally were, did these colors add or did they detract from the reality of the oil painting as oil painting. Perhaps and most likely perhaps it did not really make any difference. There was a moment though when I worried about the Courbets not being an oil painting but being a piece of country in miniature as seen in a diminishing glass. One always does like things in little. Models of furniture are nice, little flower pots are nice, little gardens are nice, penny penny peep shows are nice, magic lanterns are nice and photographs and cinemas are nice and the mirrors in front of automobiles are nice because they give the whole scene always in little and yet in natural colors like the receiver of a camera. As I say one does quite naturally like things in small, it is easy one has it all at once, and it is just like that, or in distorted mirrors when one has it even more all at once, and as I say I worried lest Courbet was like that. But soon I concluded that no, it only seemed so, no the Courbets were really oil paintings with the real life of oil paintings as oil paintings should have. Only the Courbets being nearly something else always keeps them from being really all they are. However. To come back to pictures that is oil paintings.

I began to feel that as a different thing from Courbet, nobody or nothing looked now any more like the people in the old pictures in the museums and the old pictures were alright. Did anything one saw look really like the new pictures and were they alright.

You see it gets to be a bother but still if oil paintings are oil paintings and you really like to look at them it is not really a bother.

Should a picture look like anything or does it, even a Courbet, or a Velasquez, or does it make any difference if it does or if it does not as long as it is an oil painting.

And if it is less like anything does it make any difference and if it is more like anything does it make any difference and yet if it is not like anything at all is it an oil painting.

You see it does get complicated because after all you have to like looking at an oil painting.

And then slowly through all this and looking at many many pictures I came to Cezanne and there you were, at least there I was, not all at once but as soon as I got used to it. The landscape looked like a landscape that is to say what is yellow in the landscape looked yellow in the oil painting, and what was blue in the landscape looked blue in the oil painting and if it did not there still was the oil painting, the oil painting by Cezanne. The same thing was true of the people there was no reason why it should be but it was, the same thing was true of the chairs, the same thing was true of the apples. The apples looked like apples the chairs looked like chairs and it all had nothing to do with anything because if they did not look like apples or chairs or landscape or people they were apples and chairs and landscape and people. They were so entirely these things that they were not an oil painting and yet that is just what the Cezannes were they were an oil painting. They were so entirely an oil painting that it was all there whether they were finished, the paintings, or whether they were not finished. Finished or unfinished it always was what it looked like the very essence of an oil painting because everything was always there, really there.

CEZANNE

The Irish lady can say, that to-day is every day. Caesar can say that every day is to-day and they say that every day is as they say.

In this way Cezanne nearly did nearly in this way Cezanne nearly did nearly did and nearly did. And was I surprised. Was I very surprised. Was I surprised. I was surprised and in that patient, are you patient when you find bees. Bees in a garden make a specialty of honey and so does honey. Honey and prayer. Honey and there. There where the grass can grow nearly four times yearly.

PORTRAITS AND PRAYERS—PAGE 11.

This then was a great relief to me and I began my writing.

This sounds as if it might have been an end of

something as being in the nature of a solution but it was not it was just something going on.

Up to this time I had been getting acquainted with pictures I had been intimate with a number of them but I had not been really familiar with them.

I once wrote something called Made A Mile Away, which was a description of all the pictures that had influenced me, all the pictures up to this moment the moment when I became familiar with pictures.

From this time on familiarity began and I like familiarity. It does not in me breed contempt it just breeds familiarity. And the more familiar a thing is the more there is to be familiar with. And so my familiarity began and kept on being.

From that time on I could look at any oil painting. That is the essence of familiarity that you can look at any of it.

Having thus become familiar with oil paintings I looked at any and at all of them and I looked at thousands and thousands of them. Any year in Paris if you want to look at any and all paintings you can look at thousands and thousands of them, you can look at them any day and everywhere. There are a great great many oil paintings in Paris.

Once a picture dealer told me and he knew that there were sixty thousand people in Paris painting pictures and that about twenty thousand of them were earning a living at it. There are a great many oil paintings to be seen any year in Paris.

Gradually getting more and more familiar with oil paintings was like getting gradually more and more familiar with faces as you look very hard at some of them and you look very hard at all of them and you do all of this very often. Faces gradually tell you something, there is no doubt about that as you grow more and more familiar with any and all faces and so it is with oil paintings. The result was that in a way I slowly knew what an oil painting is and gradually I realized as I had already found out very often that there is a relation between anything that is painted and the painting of it. And gradually I realized as I had found very often that that relation was so to speak nobody's business. The relation between the oil painting and the thing painted was really nobody's business. It could be the oil painting's business but actually for the purpose of the oil painting after the oil painting was painted it was not the oil painting's business and so it was nobody's business.

But still one always does like a resemblance.

A resemblance is always a pleasurable sensation and so a resemblance is almost always there.

That is not the business so to speak of the oil painting, that is just a pleasant human weakness. Anybody and so almost everybody pleasantly likes anything that resembles anything or any one.

Then there is another thing another pleasant human weakness. There is another thing about an oil painting. It makes you see something to which it is resembling makes you see the thing in the way it the oil painting resembles it. And that too and that again is a pleasant thing. But then really and this everybody knows, very soon anybody that is everybody really forgets about this resemblance. They naturally do do so because things change at least they seem so to do or any way they look as if they did change that is they look different and so the resemblance of the oil painting that is to anybody that is to anything is only a thing that has become historical.

And so we are once more back to the life in and for itself of an oil painting.

As I say having in this way become more and more familiar with any kind of an oil painting I of course became more and more familiar with many particular oil paintings with a great many particular oil paintings, and as I say when you have looked at many many faces and have become familiar with them, you may find something new in a new face you may be surprised by a different kind of a face you may be even shocked by a different kind of a face you may like or not like a new kind of a face but you cannot refuse a new face. You must accept a face as a face. And so with an oil painting. You can now see that when it came first to Matisse and then to the cubism of Picasso nothing was a bother to me. Yes of course in a way it was a bother to me but not the bother of a refusal. That would not have been possible being that I had become familiar with oil paintings, and the essence of familiarity being that you can look at any of it.

MATISSE

One was quite certain that for a long part of his being one being living he had been trying to be certain that he was wrong in doing what he was doing and then when he could not come to be certain that he had been wrong in doing what he had been doing, when he had completely convinced himself that he would not come to be certain that he had been wrong in doing what he had been doing he was really certain then that he was a great one and he certainly was a great one. Certainly every one could be certain of this thing that this one is a great one.

PORTRAITS AND PRAYERS—PAGE 12.

IF I TOLD HIM

A COMPLETED PORTRAIT OF PICASSO

If I told him would he like it. Would he like it if I told him.

Would he like it would Napoleon would Napoleon would would he like it.

If Napoleon if I told him if I told him if Napoleon. Would he like it if I told him if I told him if Napoleon. Would he like it if Napoleon if Napoleon if I told him. If I told him if Napoleon if Napoleon if I told him. If I told him would he like it would he like it if I told him.

Shutters shut and open so do queens. Shutters shut and shutters and so shutters shut and shutters and so and so shutters and so shutters shut and so shutters shut and shutters and so. And so shutters shut and so and also. And also and so and so and also. Let me recite what history teaches, History teaches.

PORTRAITS AND PRAYERS—PAGE 21

THE LIFE OF JUAN GRIS

As a Spaniard he knew cubism and had stepped through into it. He had stepped through it. There was beside this perfection. To have it shown you. Then came the war and desertion. There was little aid. Four years partly illness much perfection and rejoining beauty and perfection and then at the end there came a definite creation of something. This is what is to be measured. He made something that is to be measured. And that is that something.

PORTRAITS AND PRAYERS—PAGE 49

Anything may be a surprise to you even a shock to you but nothing can be a bother to you if you are really familiar with it. This is a natural thing.

And then having gotten so far I began often to think a great deal about oil paintings. They were familiar to me they were never really a bother to me but sometimes they were an annoyance to me.

Having now accepted all oil paintings as oil paintings I naturally sometimes began to feel something else about them. I wondered what they would be if some day they would be different. But could they be different. I often wondered in those days if oil paintings ever could be different.

This led me back to the question in oil paintings the question one might call it the eternal question for painters of oil paintings the question of the subject of the oil painting.

I naturally did not talk to painters about what they painted in their oil paintings. Painters real painters never really ever talk about that. But I told about how every picture affected me. And in a way that is what I can say. But now to go on with the difficult question why when and in which way can a painter have a subject for his pictures. And if he does and of course he does why does he. Why does he paint what he does paint.

There are first of all three things, people, objects which include flowers and fruits, landscapes which included the sea and complications of these things which may if you like be called painters' thoughts.

Beside this there are all these things staying still and then there are all these things not staying so still, even sometimes almost moving, and somehow sometime almost any painter paints them all.

And if he does is it annoying.

And is it really that that which the painter paints that in an oil painting is its element of annoyance.

Yes I think so.

Most people think that the annoyance that they feel from an oil painting that annoys them and a great many oil paintings annoy a great many people, the annoyance then that these people that anybody feels from an oil painting they think comes from the way the oil painting represents these things, the things represented in the oil painting. But I myself do not think so. I think the annoyance comes from the fact that the oil painting exists by reason of these things the oil painting represents in the oil painting, and profoundly it should not do so, so thinks the oil painting, so sometime thinks the painter of the oil painting, so instinctively feels the person looking at the oil painting. Really in everybody's heart there is a feeling of annoyance at the inevitable existence of an oil painting in relation to what it has painted people, objects and landscapes. And indeed and of course as I have already made you realize that is not what an oil painting is. An oil painting is an oil painting, and these things are only the way the only way an oil painter makes an oil painting.

One might say almost all oil painters spend their life in trying to get away from this inevitability. They struggle and the result is what everybody naturally likes or dislikes depending upon whether they think the struggle is hopeless or whether it is not. And then everybody almost everybody likes a resemblance even when there is none. Does the painter like the resemblance, oh yes he does. He does like a resemblance. That is a naturally pleasant human thing, to like a resemblance. And does this naturally pleasant human thing the liking a resemblance make everything difficult very difficult. Yes it certainly does. And it makes an oil painting annoying.

You see how this brings one to anything, to everything that any one has ever tried to do in painting.

And then there is another trouble. A painting is painted as a painting, as an oil painting existing as an oil painting, it may be in or it may be out of its frame, but an oil painting and that is a real bother always will have a tendency to go back to its frame, even if it has never been out of it. That is one of the things that an oil painting any oil painting has a very great tendency to do. And this is a bother sometimes to the painter and sometimes to any one looking at an oil painting.

Does an oil painting tend to go back into its frame because after all an oil painting belongs in its frame.

Or does it not.

It does and does not. But mostly it does and that may make for elegance that, that it does belong in its frame but it may also be a bother to the quality in it that makes it an oil painting.

And if it does belong in its frame, must it the oil painting be static.

If it tries to move and there have been good attempts to make it move does it move. Leonardo, in the Virgin child and Sainte Anne tried to make it move, Rubens in his landscapes, Picasso and Velasquez in their way, and Seurat in his way.

The trouble is always, is it the people in it who move or does the picture move and if so should it. I myself like it to do so but then I like a picture, that is an oil painting to do anything it likes to do.

The first thing that ever interested me in that way as the picture moving was the Leonardo in the Louvre, the Virgin, the child and Sainte Anne. Before this the moving in a picture was the effect of moving, but in this picture there was an internal movement, not of the people or light or any of these things but inside in the oil painting. In other words the picture did not live within the frame, in other words it did not belong within the frame. The Cezanne thing was different, it went further and further into the picture the life of the oil painting but it stayed put.

I have thought a great deal about all this and I am still thinking about it. I have passionately hoped that some picture would remain out of its frame, I think it can even while it does not, even while it remains there. And this is the problem of all modern painting just as it has been the problem of all old painting. That is to say the first hope of a painter who really feels hopeful about painting is the hope that the painting will move, that it will live outside its frame.

On the other hand most elegant painting does not move does not live outside its frame and one does like elegance in painting.

I wonder if I have at all given you an idea of what an oil painting is. I hope I have even if it does seem confused. But the confusion is essential in the idea of an oil painting.

There it is the oil painting in its frame, a thing in itself. There it is and it has to look like people or objects or landscapes. Besides that it musts not completely only exist in its frame. It must have its own life. And yet it may not move nor imitate movement, not really, nor must it stay still. It must not only be in its frame but it must not, only, be in its frame. This whole question of a picture being in its frame returning to its frame or not returning to its frame is the question that has latterly bothered me the most. Modern pictures have made the very definite effort to leave their frame. But do they stay out, do they go back and if they do is that where they belong and has anybody been deceived. I think about that a great deal these days.

You see it is difficult to describe exactly what an oil painting is, it is difficult for those who like to look at oil paintings presumably also difficult for those who paint oil paintings and it leads painters to the thing the last thing of which I wish to speak, the literary ideas so called of the painter.

I hope you all begin to feel with me what an oil painting is and granted that an oil painting is that that one likes to look at it and granted that one likes to look at it even if it is not that. Also that you do understand that what really annoys people that is anybody who is at all annoyed by an oil painting is not its being an oil painting, but the subject that is to say what it paints as an oil painting. I know I myself and mostly I am not bothered about what an oil painting has to look like am bothered by certain things oil paintings do that is by the things oil paintings always have to paint. For instance taking all the later oil paintings. Is it true that they are alright when the painting is the painting of objects and are they not alright when they are the painting of people. In spite of everything can that be a bother. May it not be a bother to you. May it not bother you. I remember so well some one saying of Van Gogh, it was a great many years ago, I like his pictures of people but not of flowers, and then adding reflectively, because of course I never do look at people and so I do not know what people look like but I do look at flowers and I do know what flowers look like. As I say persistently the thing that really annoys that deeply annoys people, that is, anybody who is annoyed by oil paintings, is not the way they are painted, that they can always get accustomed to more or less and reasonably quickly, but the subject of the oil painting. Of course it is always the same subject but even so it takes so much longer for the one looking at an oil painting to accustom himself to the subject in spite of it always being the same subject than to accustom himself to the oil painting itself. At least that is the way I feel about it.

And now there is one more subject in connection with oil paintings, the literary ideas painters have and that they paint.

The literary ideas painters have and that they paint are not at all the literary ideas writers have.

Of course the best writers that is the writers who feel writing the most as well as the best painters that is the painters who feel painting the most do not have literary ideas. But then a great many writers and a great many painters do have literary ideas. The thing that has often interested me is that the painters' literary idea is not the same kind of an idea as the writers' literary idea although they call it the same thing.

The painter has an idea which he calls a literary idea and it is to him that is he thinks it is the same kind of an idea as a writer has but it is not. And its being not makes the essential thing that makes an oil painting.

A painter's literary idea always consists not in the action but in the distortion of the form. That

could never be a writer's literary idea. Then a painter's idea of action always has to do with something
else moving rather than the center of the picture.
This is just the opposite of the writer's idea, everything else can be quiet, except the central thing which
has to move. And because of all this a painter cannot really write and a writer cannot really paint,
even fairly badly.

All this is very important because it is important.
It is important not for the painter or for the writer
but for those who like to look at paintings and who
like to know what an oil painting is and who like
to know what bothers them in what an oil painting
is. I hope I have been making it slowly clear to you.
I might have told you more in detail but in that case
you would that is to say I would not have as clearly
seen as I do now what an oil painting is.

PLAYS

IN a book I wrote called How To Write I made a discovery which I considered fundamental, that sentences are not emotional and that paragraphs are. I found out about language that paragraphs are emotional and sentences are not and I found out something else about it. I found out that this difference was not a contradiction but a combination and that this combination causes one to think endlessly about sentences and paragraphs because the emotional paragraphs are made up of unemotional sentences.

I found out a fundamental thing about plays. The thing I found out about plays was too a combination and not a contradiction and it was something that makes one think endlessly about plays.

That something is this.

The thing that is fundamental about plays is that the scene as depicted on the stage is more often than not one might say it is almost always in syncopated time in relation to the emotion of anybody in the audience.

What this says is this.

Your sensation as one in the audience in relation to the play played before you your sensation I say your emotion concerning that play is always either behind or ahead of the play at which you are looking and to which you are listening. So your emotion as a member of the audience is never going on at the same time as the action of the play.

This thing the fact that your emotional time as an audience is not the same as the emotional time of the play is what makes one endlessly troubled about a play, because not only is there a thing to know as to why this is so but also there is a thing to know why perhaps it does not need to be so.

This is a thing to know and knowledge as anybody can know is a thing to get by getting.

And so I will try to tell you what I had to get and what perhaps I have gotten in plays and to do so I will tell you all that I have ever felt about plays or about any play.

Plays are either read or heard or seen.

And there then comes the question which comes first and which is first, reading or hearing or seeing a play.

I ask you.

What is knowledge. Of course knowledge is what you know and what you know is what you do know.

What do I know about plays.

In order to know one must always go back.

What was the first play I saw and was I then already bothered bothered about the different tempo there is in the play and in yourself and your emotion in having the play go on in front of you. I think I may say I may say I know that I was already troubled by this in that my first experience at a play. The thing seen and the emotion did not go on together.

This that the thing seen and the thing felt about the thing seen not going on at the same tempo is what makes the being at the theatre something that makes anybody nervous.

The jazz bands made of this thing, the thing that makes you nervous at the theatre, they made of this thing an end in itself. They made of this different tempo a something that was nothing but a difference in tempo between anybody and everybody including all those doing it and all those hearing and seeing it. In the theatre of course this difference in tempo is less violent but still it is there and it does make anybody nervous.

In the first place at the theatre there is the curtain and the curtain already makes one feel that one is not going to have the same tempo as the thing that is there behind the curtain. The emotion of you on one side of the curtain and what is on the other side of the curtain are not going to be going on together. One will always be behind or in front of the other.

Then also beside the curtain there is the audience and the fact that they are or will be or will not be in the way when the curtain goes up that too makes for nervousness and nervousness is the certain proof that the emotion of the one seeing and the emotion of the thing seen do not progress together.

Nervousness consists in needing to go faster or to go slower so as to get together. It is that that makes anybody feel nervous.

And is it a mistake that that is what the theatre is or is it not.

There are things that are exciting as the theatre is exciting but do they make you nervous or do they not, and if they do and if they do not why do they and why do they not.

Let us think of three different kinds of things that are exciting and that make or do not make one nervous. First any scene which is a real scene something real that is happening in which one takes part as an actor in that scene. Second any book that is exciting, third the theatre at which one sees an exciting action in which one does not take part.

Now in a real scene in which one takes part at which one is an actor what does one feel as to time and what is it that does or does not make one nervous.

And is your feeling at such a time ahead and behind the action the way it is when you are at the theatre. It is the same and it is not. But more not.

If you are taking part in an actual violent scene, and you talk and they or he or she talk and it goes on and it gets more exciting and finally then it happens, whatever it is that does happen then when it happens then at the moment of happening is it a relief from the excitement or is it a completion of the excitement. In the real thing it is a completion of the excitement, in the theatre it is a relief from the excitement, and in that difference the difference between completion and relief is the difference between emotion concerning a thing seen on the stage and the emotion concerning a real presentation that is really something happening. I wish to illustrate this from a bit of The Making of Americans.

This one, and the one I am now beginning describing is Martha Hersland and this is a little story of the acting in her of her being in her very young living, this one was a very little one then and she was running and she was in the street and it was a muddy one and she had an umbrella that she was dragging and she was crying. I will throw the umbrella in the mud, she was saying, she was very little then, she was just beginning her schooling, I will throw the umbrella in the mud, she said and no one was near her and she was dragging the umbrella and bitterness possessed her, I will throw the umbrella in the mud, she was saying and nobody heard her, the others had run ahead to get home and they had left her, I will throw the umbrella in the mud, and there was desperate anger in her, I have throwed the umbrella in the mud, burst from her, she had thrown the umbrella in the mud and that was the end of it all in her. She had thrown the umbrella in the mud and no one heard her as it burst from her, I have throwed the umbrella in the mud, it was the end of all that to her.*

This then is the fundamental difference between

* THE MAKING OF AMERICANS (HARCOURT, BRACE & CO.) PAGE 232.

excitement in real life and on the stage, in real life it culminates in a sense of completion whether an exciting act or an exciting emotion has been done or not, and on the stage the exciting climax is a relief. And the memory of the two things is different. As you go over the detail that leads to culmination of any scene in real life, you find that each time you cannot get completion, but you can get relief and so already your memory of any exciting scene in which you have taken part turns it into the thing seen or heard not the thing felt. You have as I say as the result relief rather than culmination. Relief from excitement, rather than the climax of excitement. In this respect an exciting story does the same only in the exciting story, you so to speak have control of it as you have in your memory of a really exciting scene, it is not as it is on the stage a thing over which you have no real control. You can with an exciting story find out the end and so begin over again just as you can in remembering an exciting scene, but the stage is different, it is not real and yet it is not within your control as the memory of an exciting thing is or the reading of an exciting book. No matter how well you know the end of the stage story it is nevertheless not within your control as the memory of an exciting thing is or as the written story of an exciting thing is or even in a curious way the heard story of an exciting thing is. And what is the reason for this difference and what does it do to the stage. It makes for nervousness that of course, and the cause of nervousness is the fact that the emotion of the one seeing the play is always ahead or behind the play.

Beside all this there is a thing to be realised and that is how you are being introduced to the characters who take part in an exciting action even when you yourself are one of the actors. And this too has to be very much thought about. And thought about in relation to an exciting real thing to an exciting book, to an exciting theatre. How are you introduced to the characters.

There are then the three ways of having something be exciting, and the excitement may or may not make one nervous, a book being read that is exciting, a scene in which one takes part or an action in which one takes part and the theatre at which one looks on.

In each case the excitement and the nervousness and the being behind or ahead in one's feeling is different.

First anything exciting in which one takes part. There one progresses forward and back emotionally and at the supreme crisis of the scene the scene in which one takes part, in which one's hopes and loves and fears take part at the extreme crisis of this thing one is almost one with one's emotions, the action and the emotion go together, there is but just a moment of this coordination but it does exist other-

99

wise there is no completion as one has no result, no result of a scene in which one has taken part, and so instinctively when any people are living an exciting moment one with another they go on and on and on until the thing has come together the emotion the action the excitement and that is the way it is when there is any violence either of loving or hating or quarreling or losing or succeeding. But there is, there has to be the moment of it all being abreast the emotion, the excitement and the action otherwise there would be no succeeding and no failing and so no one would go on living, why yes of course not.

That is life the way it is lived.

Why yes of course and there is a reasonable and sometimes an unreasonable and very often not a reasonable amount of excitement in everybody's life and when it happens it happens in that way.

Now when you read a book how is it. Well it is not exactly like that no not even when a book is even more exciting than any excitement one has ever had. In the first place one can always look at the end of the book and so quiet down one's excitement. The excitement having been quieted down one can enjoy the excitement just as any one can enjoy the excitement of anything having happened to them by remembering and so tasting it over and over again but each time less intensely and each time until it is all over. Those who like to read books over and over get continuously this sensation of the excitement as if it were a pleasant distant thunder that rolls and rolls and the more it rolls well the further it rolls the pleasanter until it does not roll any more. That is until at last you have read the book so often that it no longer holds any excitement not even ever so faintly and then you have to wait until you have forgotten it and you can begin it again.

Now the theatre has still another way of being all this to you, the thing causing your emotion and the excitement in connection with it.

Of course lots of other things can do these things to lots of other people that is to say excite lots of people but as I have said knowledge is what you know and I naturally tell you what I know, as I do so very essentially believe in knowledge.

So then once again what does the theatre do and how does it do it.

What happens on the stage and how and how does one feel about it. That is the thing to know, to know and to tell it as so.

Is the thing seen or the thing heard the thing that makes most of its impression upon you at the theatre. How much has the hearing to do with it and how little. Does the thing heard replace the thing seen. Does it help or does it interfere with it.

And when you are taking part in something really happening that is exciting, how is it. Does the thing seen or does the thing heard effect you and effect you at the same time or in the same degree or does it not.

Can you wait to hear or can you wait to see and which excites you the most. And what has either one to do with the completion of the excitement when the excitement is a real excitement that is excited by something really happening. And then little by little does the hearing replace the seeing or does the seeing replace the hearing. Do they go together or do they not. And when the exciting something in which you have taken part arrives at its completion does the hearing replace the seeing or does it not. Does the seeing replace the hearing or does it not. Or do they both go on together.

All this is very important, and important for me and important, just important. It has of course a great deal to do with the theatre a great great deal.

In connection with reading an exciting book the thing is again more complicated than just seeing, because of course in reading one sees but one also hears and when the story is at its most exciting does one hear more than one sees or does one not do so.

I am posing all these questions to you because of course in writing, all these things are things that are really most entirely really exciting. But of course yes.

And in asking a question one is not answering but one is as one may say deciding about knowing. Knowing is what you know and in asking these questions although there is no one who answers these questions there is in them that there is knowledge. Knowledge is what you know.

And now is the thing seen or the thing heard the thing that makes most of its impression upon you at the theatre, and does as the scene on the theatre proceeds does the hearing take the place of seeing as perhaps it does when something real is being most exciting, or does seeing take the place of hearing as it perhaps does when anything real is happening or does the mixture get to be more mixed seeing and hearing as perhaps it does when anything really exciting is really happening.

If the emotion of the person looking at the theatre does or does not do what it would do if it were really a real something that was happening and they were taking part in it or they were looking at it, when the emotion of the person looking on at the theatre comes then at the climax to relief rather than completion has the mixture of seeing and hearing something to do with this and does this mixture have something to do with the nervousness of the emotion at the theatre which has perhaps to do with the fact that the emotion of the person at the theatre is always behind and ahead of the scene at the theatre but not with it.

There are then quite a number of things that any one does or does not know.

Does the thing heard replace the thing seen does it help it or does it interfere with it. Does the thing seen replace the thing heard or does it help or does it interfere with it.

I suppose one might have gotten to know a good

deal about these things from the cinema and how it changed from sight to sound, and how much before there was real sound how much of the sight was sound or how much it was not. In other words the cinema undoubtedly had a new way of understanding sight and sound in relation to emotion and time.

I may say that as a matter of fact the thing which has induced a person like myself to constantly think about the theatre from the standpoint of sight and sound and its relation to emotion and time, rather than in relation to story and action is the same as you may say general form of conception as the inevitable experiments made by the cinema although the method of doing so has naturally nothing to do with the other. I myself never go to the cinema or hardly ever practically never and the cinema has never read my work or hardly ever. The fact remains that there is the same impulse to solve the problem of time in relation to emotion and the relation of the scene to the emotion of the audience in the one case as in the other. There is the same impulse to solve the problem of the relation of seeing and hearing in the one case as in the other.

It is in short the inevitable problem of anybody living in the composition of the present time, that is living as we are now living as we have it and now do live in it.

The business of Art as I tried to explain in Composition as Explanation is to live in the actual present, that is the complete actual present, and to completely express that complete actual present.

But to come back to that other question which is at once so important a part of any scene in real life, in books or on the stage, how are the actors introduced to the sight, hearing and consciousness of the person having the emotion about them. How is it done in each case and what has that to do with the way the emotion progresses.

How are the actors in a real scene introduced to those acting with them in that scene and how are the real actors in a real scene introduced to you who are going to be in an exciting scene with them. How does it happen, that is, as it usually happens.

And how are the actors in a book scene introduced to the reader of the book, how does one come to know them, that is how is one really introduced to them.

And how are the people on the stage that is the people the actors act how are they introduced to the audience and what is the reason why, the reason they are introduced in the way that they are introduced, and what happens, and how does it matter, and how does it affect the emotions of the audience.

In a real scene, naturally in a real scene, you either have already very well known all the actors in the real scene of which you are one, or you have not. More generally you have than you have not, but and this is the element of excitement in an exciting scene, it quite of course is the element of excitement in an exciting scene that is in a real scene, all that you have known of the persons including yourself who are taking part in the exciting scene, although you have most probably known them very well, what makes it exciting is that insofar as the scene is exciting they the actors in the scene including yourself might just as well have been strangers because they all act talk and feel differently from the way you have expected them to act feel or talk. And this that they feel act and talk including yourself differently from the way you would have thought that they would act feel and talk makes the scene an exciting scene and makes the climax of this scene which is a real scene a climax of completion and not a climax of relief. That is what a real scene is. Would it make any difference in a real scene if they were all strangers, if they had never known each other. Yes it would, it would be practically impossible in the real scene to have a really exciting scene if they were all strangers because generally speaking it is the contradiction between the way you know the people you know including yourself act and the way they are acting or feeling or talking that makes of any scene that is an exciting scene an exciting scene.

Of course there are other exciting scenes in peace and in war in which the exciting scene takes place with strangers but in that case for the purpose of excitement you are all strangers but so completely strangers, including you yourself to yourself as well as the others to each other and to you that they are not really individuals and inasmuch as that is so it has the advantage and the disadvantage that you proceed by a series of completions which follow each other so closely that when it is all over you cannot remember that is you cannot really reconstruct the thing, the thing that has happened. That is something that one must think about in relation to the theatre and it is a very interesting thing. Then in a case like that where you are all strangers in an exciting scene what happens as far as hearing and seeing is concerned. When in an exciting scene where you are all strangers you to yourself and you to them and they to you and they to each other and where no one of all of them including yourself have any consciousness of knowing each other do you have the disadvantage of not knowing the difference between hearing and seeing and is that a disadvantage from the standpoint of remembering. From that standpoint the standpoint of remembering it is a serious disadvantage.

But we may say that that exciting experience of exciting scenes where you have really no acquaintance with the other actors as well as none with yourself in an exciting action are comparatively rare and are not the normal material of excitement as it is exciting in the average person's experience.

As I say in the kind of excitement where you have had no normal introduction to the actors of the scene the action and the emotion is so violent that sight sound and emotion is so little realized that it cannot be remembered and therefore in a kind of a way it has really nothing to do with anything because really it is more exciting action than exciting emotion or excitement. I think I can say that these are not the same thing. Have they anything to do with the way the theatre gets you to know or not to know what the people on the stage are. Perhaps yes and perhaps no.

In ordinary life one has known pretty well the people with whom one is having the exciting scene before the exciting scene takes place and one of the most exciting elements in the excitement be it love or a quarrel or a struggle is that, that having been well known that is familiarly known, they all act in acting violently act in the same way as they always did of course only the same way has become so completely different that from the standpoint of familiar acquaintance there is none there is complete familiarity but there is no proportion that has hitherto been known, and it is this which makes the scene the real scene exciting, and it is this that leads to completion, the proportion achieves in your emotion the new proportion therefore it is completion but not relief. A new proportion cannot be a relief.

Now how does one naturally get acquainted in real life which makes one have a familiarity with some one. By a prolonged familiarity of course.

And how does one achieve this familiarity with the people in a book or the people on the stage. Or does one.

108

In real life the familiarity is of course the result of accident, intention or natural causes but in any case there is a progressive familiarity that makes one acquainted.

Now in a book there is an attempt to do the same thing that is, to say, to do a double thing, to make the people in the book familiar with each other and to make the reader familiar with them. That is the reason in a book it is always a strange doubling, the familiarity between the characters in the book is a progressive familiarity and the familiarity between them and the reader is a familiarity that is a forcing process or an incubation. It makes of course a double time and later at another time we will go into that.

But now how about the theatre.

It is not possible in the theatre to produce familiarity which is of the essence of acquaintance because, in the first place when the actors are there they are there and they are there right away.

When one reads a play and very often one does read a play, anyway one did read Shakespeare's play a great deal at least I did, it was always necessary to keep one's finger in the list of characters for at least the whole first act, and in a way it is necessary to do the same when the play is played. One has one's programme for that and beside one has to become or has become acquainted with the actors as an actor and one has one's programme too for that. And so the introduction to the characters on the stage has a great many different sides to it. And this has again a great deal to do with the nervousness of the theatre excitement.

Anybody who was as I was, brought up and at the time that I was brought up was brought up in Oakland and in San Francisco inevitably went to the theatre a lot. Actors in those days liked to go out to the Coast and as it was expensive to get back and not expensive to stay there they stayed. Besides that there were a great many foreign actors who came and having come stayed and any actor who stays acts and so there was always a great deal to see on the stage and children went, they went with each other and they went alone, and they went with people who were older, and there was twenty-five cent opera to which anybody went and the theatre was natural and anybody went to the theatre. I did go a great deal in those days. I also read plays a great deal. I rather liked reading plays, I very much liked reading plays. In the first place there was in reading plays as I have said the necessity of going forward and back to the list of characters to find out which was which and then insensibly to know. Then there was the poetry and then gradually there were the portraits.

I can remember quite definitely in the reading of plays that there were very decidedly these three things, the way of getting acquainted that was not an imitation of what one usually did, but the having to remember which character was which. That was very different from real life or from a book. Then there was the element of poetry. Poetry connected with a play was livelier poetry than poetry unconnected with a play. In the first place there were a great many bits that were short and sometimes it was only a line.

I remember Henry the Sixth which I read and re-read and which of course I have never seen played but which I liked to read because there were so many characters and there were so many little bits in it that were lively words. In the poetry of plays words are more lively words than in any other kind of poetry and if one naturally liked lively words and I naturally did one likes to read plays in poetry. I always as a child read all the plays I could get hold of that were in poetry. Plays in prose do not read so well. The words in prose are livelier when they are not a play. I am not saying anything about why, it is just a fact.

So then for me there was the reading of plays which was one thing and then there was the seeing of plays and of operas a great many of them which was another thing.

Later on so very much later on there was for me the writing of plays which was one thing and there was at that time no longer any seeing of plays. I practically when I wrote my first play had completely ceased going to the theatre. In fact although I have written a great many plays and I am quite sure they are plays I have since I commenced writing these plays I have practically never been inside of any kind of a theatre.

111

Of course none of this has been intentional, one may say generally speaking that anything that is really inevitable, that is to say necessary is not intentional.

But to go back to the plays I did see, and then to go on to the plays I did write.

It was then a natural thing in the Oakland and San Francisco in which I was brought up to see a great many plays played. Beside there was a great deal of opera played and so all of it was natural enough and how did I feel about it.

Generally speaking all the early recollections all a child's feeling of the theatre is two things. One which is in a way like a circus that is the general movement and light and air which any theatre has, and a great deal of glitter in the light and a great deal of height in the air, and then there are moments, a very very few moments but still moments. One must be pretty far advanced in adolescence before one realizes a whole play.

Up to the time of adolescence when one does really live in a whole play up to that time the theatre consists of bright filled space and usually not more than one moment in a play.

I think this is fairly everybody's experience and it was completely mine.

Uncle Tom's Cabin may not have been my first play but it was very nearly my first play. I think my first play really was Pinafore in London but the theatre there was so huge that I do not remember at all seeing a stage I only remember that it felt like a theatre that is the theatre did. I doubt if I did see the stage.

In Uncle Tom's Cabin I remember only the escape across the ice, I imagine because the blocks of ice moving up and down naturally would catch my eye more than the people on the stage would.

The next thing was the opera the twenty-five cent opera of San Francisco and the fight in Faust. But that I imagine was largely because my brother had told me about the fight in Faust. As a matter of fact I gradually saw more of the opera because I saw it quite frequently. Then there was Buffalo Bill and the Indian attack, well of course anybody raised where everybody collected arrow heads and played Indians would notice Indians. And then there was Lohengrin, and there all that I saw was the swan being changed into a boy, our insisting on seeing that made my father with us lose the last boat home to Oakland, but my brother and I did not mind, naturally not as it was the moment.

In spite of my having seen operas quite often the first thing that I remember as sound on the stage was the playing by some English actor of Richelieu at the Oakland theatre and his repeated calling out, Nemours Nemours. That is the first thing that I remember hearing with my ears at the theatre and as I say nothing is more interesting to know about the theatre than the relation of sight and sound. It is always the most interesting thing about anything to know whether you hear or you see. And how one has to do with the other. It is one of the important things in finding out how you know what you know.

Then I enormously remember Booth playing Hamlet but there again the only thing I noticed and it is rather a strange thing to have noticed is his lying at the Queen's feet during the play. One would suppose that a child would notice other things in the play than that but that is what I remember and I noticed him there more than I did the play he saw, although I knew that there was a play going on there, that is the little play. It was in this way that I first felt two things going on at one time. That is something that one has to come to feel.

Then the next thing I knew was adolescence and going to the theatre all the time, a great deal alone, and all of it making an outside inside existence for me, not so real as books, which were all inside me, but so real that it the theatre made me real outside of me which up to that time I never had been in my emotion. I had largely been so in an active daily life but not in any emotion.

Then gradually there came the beginning of really realising the great difficulty of having my emotion accompany the scene and then moreover I became fairly consciously troubled by the things over which one stumbles over which one stumbled to such an extent that the time of one's emotion in relation to the scene was always interrupted. The things over

114

which one stumbled and there it was a matter both of seeing and of hearing were clothes, voices, what they the actors said, how they were dressed and how that related itself to their moving around. Then the bother of never being able to begin over again because before it had commenced it was over, and at no time had you been ready, either to commence or to be over. Then I began to vaguely wonder whether I could see and hear at the same time and which helped or interfered with the other and which helped or interfered with the thing on the stage having been over before it really commenced. Could I see and hear and feel at the same time and did I.

I began to be a good deal troubled by all these things, the more emotion I felt while at the theatre the more troubled I became by all these things.

And then I was relieved.

As I said San Francisco was a wonderful place to hear and see foreign actors as at that time they liked it when they got there and they stayed and they played.

I must have been about sixteen years old and Bernhardt came to San Francisco and stayed two months. I knew a little french of course but really it did not matter, it was all so foreign and her voice being so varied and it all being so french I could rest in it untroubled. And I did.

It was better than the opera because it went on. It was better than the theatre because you did not have to get acquainted. The manners and customs of the french theatre created a thing in itself and it existed in and for itself as the poetical plays had that I used so much to read, there were so many characters just as there were in those plays and you did not have to know them they were so foreign, and the foreign scenery and actuality replaced the poetry and the voices replaced the portraits. It was for me a very simple direct and moving pleasure.

This experience curiously enough and yet perhaps it was not so curious awakened in me a desire for melodrama on the stage, because there again everything happened so quietly one did not have to get acquainted and as what the people felt was of no importance one did not have to realize what was said.

This pleasure in melodrama and in those days there was always one theatre in a theatrically inclined town that played melodrama, this pleasure in melodrama culminated for me in the civil war dramas of that period and the best of them was of course Secret Service. Gillette had conceived a new technique, silence stillness and quick movement. Of course it had been done in the melodrama already by the villains particularly in such plays as the Queen of Chinatown and those that had to do with telegraph operators. But Gillette had not only done it but he had conceived it and it made the whole stage the whole play this technique silence stillness and quick movement. One was no longer bothered by the theatre, you had to get acquainted of course but that was quickly over and after that nothing bothered. In fact Gillette created what the cinema later repeated by mixing up the short story and the stage but there is yet the trouble with the cinema that it is after all a photograph, and a photograph continues to be a photograph and yet can it become something else. Perhaps it can but that is a whole other question. If it can then some one will have to feel that about it. But to go on.

From then on I was less and less interested in the theatre.

I became more interested in opera, I went one went and the whole business almost came together and then finally, just finally, I came not to care at all for music and so having concluded that music was made for adolescents and not for adults and having just left adolescence behind me and beside I knew all the operas anyway by that time I did not care any more for opera.

Then I came to Paris to live and there for a long time I did not go to the theatre at all. I forgot the theatre, I never thought about the theatre. I did sometimes think about the opera. I went to the opera once in Venice and I liked it and then much later Strauss' Electra made me realize that in a kind of a way there could be a solution of the problem of conversation on the stage. Beside it was a new opera and it is quite exciting to hear something unknown really unknown.

But as I say I settled down to Paris life and I forgot

the theatre and almost forgot opera. There was of course Isadora Duncan and then the Russian ballet and in between Spain and the Argentine and bull-fights and I began once more to feel something about something going on at a theatre.

And then I went back, not in my reading but in my feeling to the reading of plays in my childhood, the lots of characters, the poetry and the portraits and the scenery which was always of course and ought always to be of course woods that is forests and trees and streets and windows.

And so one day all of a sudden I began to write Plays.

I remember very well the first one I wrote. I called it What Happened, a Play, it is in Geography and Plays as are all the plays I wrote at that time. I think and always have thought that if you write a play you ought to announce that it is a play and that is what I did. What Happened. A Play.

I had just come home from a pleasant dinner party and I realized then as anybody can know that something is always happening.

Something is always happening, anybody knows a quantity of stories of people's lives that are always happening, there are always plenty for the newspapers and there are always plenty in private life. Everybody knows so many stories and what is the use of telling another story. What is the use of telling a story since there are so many and everybody knows so many and tells so many. In the country it is perfectly extraordinary how many complicated dramas go on all the time. And everybody knows them, so why tell another one. There is always a story going on.

So naturally what I wanted to do in my play was what everybody did not always know nor always tell. By everybody I do of course include myself by always I do of course include myself.

And so I wrote, What Happened, A Play.

Then I wrote Ladies Voices and then I wrote a Curtain Raiser. I did this last because I wanted still more to tell what could be told if one did not tell anything.

Perhaps I will read some of these to you later.

Then I went to Spain and there I wrote a lot of plays. I concluded that anything that was not a story could be a play and I even made plays in letters and advertisements.

I had before I began writing plays written many portraits. I had been enormously interested all my life in finding out what made each one that one and so I had written a great many portraits.

I came to think that since each one is that one and that there are a number of them each one being that one, the only way to express this thing each one being that one and there being a number of them knowing each other was in a play. And so I began to write these plays. And the idea in What Happened, A Play was to express this without telling what happened, in short to make a play the essence of what happened.

I tried to do this with the first series of plays that I wrote.

A tiger a rapt and surrounded overcoat securely arranged with spots old enough to be thought useful and witty quite witty in a secret and in a blinding flurry.*

ACT TWO

(Three)

Four and nobody wounded, five and nobody flourishing, six and nobody talkative, eight and nobody sensible.

One and a left hand lift that is so heavy that there is no way of pronouncing perfectly.

A point of accuracy, a point of a strange stove, a point that is so sober that the reason left is all the chance of swelling.

(The same three.)

A wide oak a wide enough oak, a very wide cake, a lightning cooky, a single wide open and exchanged box filled with the same little sac that shines.

The best the only better and more left footed stranger.

The very kindness there is in all lemons oranges apples pears and potatoes.

(The same three.)

* GEOGRAPHY AND PLAYS (FOUR SEAS CO.) PAGE 205.

120

A same frame a sadder portal, a singular gate and a bracketed mischance.

A rich market where there is no memory of more moon than there is everywhere and yet where strangely there is apparel and a whole set.

A connection, a clam cup connection, a survey, a ticket and a return to laying over.

ACT THREE

(Two.)

A cut, a cut is not a slice, what is the occasion for representing a cut and a slice. What is the occasion for all that.

A cut is a slice, a cut is the same slice. The reason that a cut is a slice is that if there is no hurry any time is just as useful.*

I have of course always been struggling with this thing, to say what you nor I nor nobody knows, but what is really what you and I and everybody knows, and as I say everybody hears stories but the thing that makes each one what he is is not that. Everybody hears stories and knows stories. How can they not because that is what anybody does and what everybody tells. But in my portraits I had tried to tell what each one is without telling stories and now in my early plays I tried to tell what happened without telling

* GEOGRAPHY AND PLAYS. PAGE 206.

stories so that the essence of what happened would be like the essence of the portraits, what made what happened be what it was. And then I had for the moment gone as far as I could then go in plays and I went back to poetry and portraits and description.

Then I began to spend my summers in Bilignin in the department of the Ain and there I lived in a landscape that made itself its own landscape. I slowly came to feel that since the landscape was the thing, I had tried to write it down in Lucy Church Amiably and I did but I wanted it even more really, in short I found that since the landscape was the thing, a play was a thing and I went on writing plays a great many plays. The landscape at Bilignin so completely made a play that I wrote quantities of plays.

I felt that if a play was exactly like a landscape then there would be no difficulty about the emotion of the person looking on at the play being behind or ahead of the play because the landscape does not have to make acquaintance. You may have to make acquaintance with it, but it does not with you, it is there and so the play being written the relation between you at any time is so exactly that that it is of no importance unless you look at it. Well I did look at it and the result is in all the plays that I have printed as Operas and Plays.

MARIUS.   I am very pleased I am indeed very pleased that it is a great pleasure.

MARTHA. If four are sitting at a table and one of them is lying upon it it does not make any difference. If bread and pomegranates are on a table and four are sitting at the table and one of them is leaning upon it it does not make any difference.

MARTHA. It does not make any difference if four are seated at a table and one is leaning upon it.

MARYAS. If five are seated at a table and there is bread on it and there are pomegranates on it and one of the five is leaning on the table it does not make any difference.

MARTHA. If on a day that comes again and if we consider a day a week day it does come again if on a day that comes again and we consider every day to be a day that comes again it comes again then when accidentally when very accidentally every other day and every other day every other day and every other day that comes again and every day comes again when accidentally every other day comes again, every other day comes again and every other and every day comes again and accidentally and every day and it comes again, a day

123

comes again and a day in that way comes again.

MARYAS. Accidentally in the morning and after that every evening and accidentally every evening and after that every morning and after that accidentally every morning and after that accidentally and after that every morning.

MARYAS. After that accidentally. Accidentally after that.

MARYAS. Accidentally after that. After that accidentally.

MARYAS.
AND
MARTHA. More Maryas and more Martha.

MARYAS.
AND
MARTHA. More Martha and more Maryas.

MARTHA.
AND
MARYAS. More and more and more Martha and more Maryas.

MARIUS. It is spoken of in that way.

MABEL. It is spoken of in that way.

MARIUS
AND
MABEL. It is spoken in that way and it is spoken of in that way.

MARIUS
AND
MABEL. It is spoken of in that way.

124

MABEL.	I speak of it in that way.
MARIUS.	I have spoken of it in that way and I speak it in that way. I have spoken of it in that way.
MABEL.	I speak of it in that way.*

The landscape has its formation and as after all a play has to have formation and be in relation one thing to the other thing and as the story is not the thing as any one is always telling something then the landscape not moving but being always in relation, the trees to the hills the hills to the fields the trees to each other any piece of it to any sky and then any detail to any other detail, the story is only of importance if you like to tell or like to hear a story but the relation is there anyway. And of that relation I wanted to make a play and I did, a great number of plays.

SAY IT WITH FLOWERS

A PLAY

George Henry, Henry Henry and Elisabeth
Henry.
Subsidiary characters.
Elisabeth and William Long.
Time Louis XI
Place Gisors.
Action in a cake shop and the sea shore.
Other interests.

* OPERAS AND PLAYS (PLAIN EDITION) RANDOM HOUSE. PAGE 92.

The welcoming of a man and his dog and the
wish that they would come back sooner.
George Henry and Elisabeth Henry and Henry
Henry ruminating.

Elisabeth and William Long.

Waiting.

Who has asked them to be amiable to me.

She said she was waiting.

George Henry and Elisabeth Henry and
Henry Henry.

Who might be asleep if they were not waiting
for me.

She.

Elisabeth Henry and Henry Henry and
George Henry.

She might be waiting with me.

Henry Henry absolutely ready to be here with
me.

Scenery.

The home where they were waiting for William
Long to ask them to come along and ask them not
to be waiting for them.

Will they be asleep while they are waiting.

They will be pleased with everything.

What is everything.

A hyacinth is everything.

Will they be sleeping while they are waiting for
everything.

William Long and Elisabeth Long were so

silent you might have heard an egg shell breaking. They were busy all day long with everything.

Elisabeth and William Long were very busy waiting for him to come and bring his dog along.

Why did they not go with him.

Because they were busy waiting.*

LOUIS XI AND MADAME GIRAUD
Scene II
Louis the XI loved a boat
A boat on the Seine
Sinks and leaves.
Leaves which have patterns
They with delight.
Make it be loaned
To administer their confinement
They will go away
Without which it will matter.
Louis XI
Has won gold for France
And in this way.
He has settled she and a girl
He and a wife
He and a friend
They and their mother
The mother and the son Percy.†

* OPERAS AND PLAYS. PAGE 331.
† OPERAS AND PLAYS. PAGE 352.

MADAME RECAMIER

Yvonne Marin

Out loud is when the mother wishes
When the brother fishes
When the father considers wishes
When the sister supposes wishes
She will change to say I say I say so.
Let her think of learning nothing.
Let her think of seeing everything
Let her think like that.

Florence Descotes

Never to be restless
Never to be afraid
Never to ask will they come
Never to have made
Never to like having had
Little that is left then
She made it do
One and two
Thank her for everything.

Madame Recamier

It is not thoughtless to think well of them.

Louis Raynal

A place where she sits
Is a place where they were *

The only one of course that has been played is Four
Saints. In Four Saints I made the Saints the land-

* OPERAS AND PLAYS. PAGE 365.

scape. All the saints that I made and I made a number of them because after all a great many pieces of things are in a landscape all these saints together made my landscape. These attendant saints were the landscape and it the play really is a landscape.

A landscape does not move nothing really moves in a landscape but things are there, and I put into the play the things that were there.

Magpies are in the landscape that is they are in the sky of a landscape, they are black and white and they are in the sky of the landscape in Bilignin and in Spain, especially in Avila. When they are in the sky they do something that I have never seen any other bird do they hold themselves up and down and look flat against the sky.

A very famous French inventor of things that have to do with stabilisation in aviation told me that what I told him magpies did could not be done by any bird but anyway whether the magpies at Avila do do it or do not at least they look as if they do do it. They look exactly like the birds in the Annunciation pictures the bird which is the Holy Ghost and rests flat against the side sky very high.

There were magpies in my landscape and there were scarecrows.

The scarecrows on the ground are the same thing as the magpies in the sky, they are a part of the landscape.

They the magpies may tell their story if they and

you like or even if I like but stories are only stories but that they stay in the air is not a story but a landscape. That scarecrows stay on the ground is the same thing it could be a story but it is a piece of the landscape.

Then as I said streets and windows are also landscape and they added to my Spanish landscape.

While I was writing the Four Saints I wanted one always does want the saints to be actually saints before them as well as inside them, I had to see them as well as feel them. As it happened there is on the Boulevard Raspail a place where they make photographs that have always held my attention. They take a photograph of a young girl dressed in the costume of her ordinary life and little by little in successive photographs they change it into a nun. These photographs are small and the thing takes four or five changes but at the end it is a nun and this is done for the family when the nun is dead and in memoriam. For years I had stood and looked at these when I was walking and finally when I was writing Saint Therese in looking at these photographs I saw how Saint Therese existed from the life of an ordinary young lady to that of the nun. And so everything was actual and I went on writing.

Then in another window this time on the rue de Rennes there was a rather large porcelain group and it was of a young soldier giving alms to a beggar and taking off his helmet and his armour and leaving them in the charge of another.

It was somehow just what the young Saint Ignatius did and anyway it looked like him as I had known about him and so he too became actual not as actual as Saint Therese in the photographs but still actual and so the Four Saints got written.

All these things might have been a story but as a landscape they were just there and a play is just there. That is at least the way I feel about it.

Anyway I did write Four Saints an Opera to be Sung and I think it did almost what I wanted, it made a landscape and the movement in it was like a movement in and out with which anybody looking on can keep in time. I also wanted it to have the movement of nuns very busy and in continuous movement but placid as a landscape has to be because after all the life in a convent is the life of a landscape, it may look excited a landscape does sometimes look excited but its quality is that a landscape if it ever did go away would have to go away to stay.

Anyway the play as I see it is exciting and it moves but it also stays and that is as I said in the beginning might be what a play should do.

Anyway I am pleased. People write me that they are having a good time while the opera is going on a thing which they say does not very often happen to them at the theatre.

So you do see what I have after all meant.

And so this is just at present all I know about the theatre.

THE GRADUAL MAKING
OF
THE MAKING OF
AMERICANS

I AM going to read what I have written to read, because in a general way it is easier even if it is not better and in a general way it is better even if it is not easier to read what has been written than to say what has not been written. Any way that is one way to feel about it.

And I want to tell you about the gradual way of making The Making of Americans. I made it gradually and it took me almost three years to make it, but that is not what I mean by gradual. What I mean by gradual is the way the preparation was made inside of me. Although as I tell it it will sound historical, it really is not historical as I still very much remember it. I do remember it. That is I can remember it. And if you can remember, it may be history but it is not historical.

To begin with, I seem always to be doing the talking when I am anywhere but in spite of that I do listen. I always listen. I always have listened. I always have listened to the way everybody has to tell what they have to say. In other words I always have listened in my way of listening until they have told me and told me until I really know it, that is know what they are.

I always as I admit seem to be talking but talking can be a way of listening that is if one has the profound need of hearing and seeing what every one is telling.

And I began very early in life to talk all the time and to listen all the time. At least that is the way I feel about it.

I cannot remember not talking all the time and all the same feeling that while I was talking while I was seeing that I was not only hearing but seeing while I was talking and that at the same time the relation between myself knowing I was talking and those to whom I was talking and incidentally to whom I was listening were coming to tell me and tell me in their way everything that made them.

Those of you who have read The Making of Americans I think will very certainly understand.

When I was young and I am talking of a period even before I went to college part of this talking consisted in a desire not only to hear what each one was saying in every way everybody has of saying it but also then of helping to change them and to help them change themselves.

I was very full of convictions in those days and I at that time thought that the passion I had for finding out by talking and listening just how everybody was always telling everything that was inside them that made them that one, that this passion for knowing the basis of existence in each one was in me to help them change themselves to become what they should become. The changing should of course be dependent upon my ideas and theirs theirs as much as mine at that time.

And so in those early days I wanted to know what was inside each one which made them that one and I was deeply convinced that I needed this to help them change something.

Then I went to college and there for a little while I was tremendously occupied with finding out what was inside myself to make me what I was. I think that does happen to one at that time. It had been happening before going to college but going to college made it more lively. And being so occupied with what made me myself inside me, made me perhaps not stop talking but for awhile it made me stop listening.

At any rate that is the way it seems to me now looking back at it.

While I was at college and doing philosophy and psychology I became more and more interested in my own mental and physical processes and less in that of others and all I then was learning of what made people what they were came to me by experience and not by talking and listening.

Then as I say I became more interested in psychology, and one of the things I did was testing reactions of the average college student in a state of normal activity and in the state of fatigue induced by their examinations. I was supposed to be interested in their reactions but soon I found that I was not but instead that I was enormously interested in the types of their characters that is what I even then thought of as the bottom nature of them, and when in May 1898 I wrote my half of the report of these experiments I expressed these results as follows:

In these descriptions it will be readily observed that habits of attention are reflexes of the complete character of the individual.

Then that was over and I went to the medical school where I was bored and where once more myself and my experiences were more actively interesting me than the life inside of others.

But then after that once more I began to listen, I had left the medical school and I had for the moment nothing to do but talk and look and listen, and I did this tremendously.

I then began again to think about the bottom nature in people, I began to get enormously interested in hearing how everybody said the same thing over and over again with infinite variations but over and over again until finally if you listened with great intensity you could hear it rise and fall and tell all that that there was inside them, not so much by the actual words they said or the thoughts they had but the movement of their thoughts and words endlessly the same and endlessly different.

Many things then come out in the repeating that make a history of each one for any one who always listens to them. Many things come out of each one and as one listens to them listens to all the repeating in them, always this comes to be clear about them, the history of them of the bottom nature in them, the nature or natures mixed up in them to make the whole of them in anyway it mixes up in them. Sometime then there will be a history of every one.

When you come to feel the whole of anyone from the beginning to the ending, all the kind of repeating there is in them, the different ways at different times repeating comes out of them, all the kinds of things and mixtures in each one, anyone can see then by looking hard at any one living near them that a history of every one must be a long one. A history of any one must be a long one, slowly it comes out from them from their beginning to their ending, slowly you can see it in them the nature and the mixtures in them, slowly everything comes out from each one in the kind of repeating each one does in the different parts and kinds of living they have in them, slowly then the history of them comes out from them, slowly then any one who looks well at any one will have the history of the whole of that one. Slowly the history of each one comes out of each one. Sometime then there will be a history of every one. Mostly every history will be a long one. Slowly it comes out of each one, slowly any one who looks at them gets the history of each part of the living of any one in the history

of the whole of each one that sometime there will
be of every one.

THE MAKING OF AMERICANS (HARCOURT, BRACE
& CO.) PAGE 128.

Repeating then is in every one, in every one
their being and their feeling and their way of
realizing everything and every one comes out of
them in repeating. More and more then every one
comes to be clear to some one.

Slowly every one in continuous repeating, to
their minutest variation, comes to be clearer to
some one. Every one who ever was or is or will be
living sometimes will be clearly realized by some
one. Sometime there will be an ordered history
of every one. Slowly every kind of one comes into
ordered recognition. More and more then it is
wonderful in living the subtle variations coming
clear into ordered recognition, coming to make
every one a part of some kind of them, some kind
of men and women. Repeating then is in every
one, every one then comes sometime to be clearer
to some one, sometime there will be then an or-
derly history of every one who ever was or is or
will be living.

THE MAKING OF AMERICANS.

Then I became very interested in resemblances, in
resemblances and slight differences between people. I

began to make charts of all the people I had ever known or seen, or met or remembered.

Every one is always busy with it, no one of them then ever want to know it that every one looks like some one else and they see it mostly every one dislikes to hear it. It is very important to me to always know it, to always see it which one looks like others and to tell it.—The Making of Americans, page 211. I write for myself and strangers, I do this for my own sake and for the sake of those who know I know it that they look like other ones, that they are separate and yet always repeated. There are some who like it that I know they are like many others and repeat it, there are many who never can really like it.

Every one is one inside them, every one reminds some one of some other one who is or was or will be living. Every one has it to say of each one he is like such a one I see it in him, every one has it to say of each one she is like some one else I can tell by remembering. So it goes on always in living, every one is always remembering some one who is resembling to the one at whom they are then looking. So they go on repeating, every one is themselves inside them and every one is resembling to others and that is always interesting.

THE MAKING OF AMERICANS, PAGE 212.

141

I began to see that as I saw when I saw so many students at college that all this was gradually taking form. I began to get very excited about it. I began to be sure that if I could only go on long enough and talk and hear and look and see and feel enough and long enough I could finally describe really describe every kind of human being that ever was or is or would be living.

I got very wrapped up in all this. And I began writing The Making of Americans.

Let me read you some passages to show you how passionately and how desperately I felt about all this.

I am altogether a discouraged one. I am just now altogether a discouraged one. I am going on describing men and women.

THE MAKING OF AMERICANS, PAGE 308.

I have been very glad to have been wrong. It is sometimes a very hard thing to win myself to having been wrong about something. I do a great deal of suffering.

THE MAKING OF AMERICANS, PAGE 310.

I was sure that in a kind of a way the enigma of the universe could in this way be solved. That after all description is explanation, and if I went on and on and on enough I could describe every individual human being that could possibly exist. I did proceed to do as much as I could.

Some time then there will be very kind of a history of every one who ever can or is or was or will be living. Some time then there will be a history of every one from their beginning to their ending. Sometime then there will be a history of all of them, of every kind of them, of every one, of every bit of living they ever have in them, of them when there is never more than a beginning to them, of every kind of them, of every one when there is very little beginning and then there is an ending, there will then sometime be a history of every one there will be a history of everything that ever was or is or will be them, of everything that was or is or will be all of any one or all of all of them. Sometime then there will be a history of every one, of everything or anything that is all them or any part of them and sometime then there will be a history of how anything or everything comes out from every one, comes out from every one or any one from the beginning to the ending of the being in them. Sometime then there must be a history of every one who ever was or is or will be living. As one sees every one in their living, in their loving, sitting, eating, drinking, sleeping, walking, working, thinking, laughing, as any one sees all of them from their beginning to their ending, sees them when they are little babies or children or young grown men and women or growing older men and women or old men and women then one knows it in them that sometime there will be a history of all of them, that sometime all of them will have the last touch of being, a history of them can give to them, sometime then there will be a history of each one, of all the kinds of them, of all the ways any one can know them, of all the ways each one is inside her or inside him, of all the ways anything of them comes out from them. Sometime then there will be a history of every one and so then every one will have in them the last touch of being a history of any one can give to them.

THE MAKING OF AMERICANS, PAGE 124.

This is then a beginning of the way of knowing everything in every one, of knowing the complete history of each one who ever is or was or will be living. This is then a little description of the winning of so much wisdom.

THE MAKING OF AMERICANS, PAGE 217.

Of course all the time things were happening that is in respect to my hearing and seeing and feeling. I found that as often as I thought and had every reason to be certain that I had included everything in my knowledge of any one something else would turn up that had to be included. I did not with this get at all discouraged I only became more and more interested. And I may say that I am still more and more interested I find as many things to be added now as ever and that does make it eternally interesting. So I found myself getting deeper and deeper into the idea of describing really describing every individual that could exist.

While I was doing all this all unconsciously at the same time a matter of tenses and sentences came to fascinate me.

While I was listening and hearing and feeling the rhythm of each human being I gradually began to feel the difficulty of putting it down. Types of people I could put down but a whole human being felt at one and the same time, in other words while in the act of feeling that person was very difficult to put into words.

And so about the middle of The Making of Americans I became very consciously obsessed by this very definite problem.

It happens very often that a man has it in him, that a man does something, that he does it very often that he does many things, when he is a young man when he is an old man, when he is an older man. One of such of these kind of them had a little boy and this one, the little son wanted to make a collection of butterflies and beetles and it was all exciting to him and it was all arranged then and then the father said to the son you are certain this is not a cruel thing that you are wanting to be doing, killing things to make collections of them, and the son was very disturbed then and they talked about it together the two of them and more and more they talked about it then and then at last the boy was convinced it was a cruel thing and he said he would not do it and his father said the little boy was a noble boy to give up pleasure when it was a cruel one. The boy went to bed then and then the father when he got up in the early morning saw a wonderfully beautiful moth in the room and he caught him and he killed him and he pinned him and he woke up his son then and showed it to him and he said to him see what a good father I am to have caught and killed this one, the boy was all mixed up inside him and then he said he would go on with his collecting and that was all there was then of discussing and this is a little description of something that happened once and it is very interesting.

THE MAKING OF AMERICANS, PAGE 284.

And this brings us to the question of grammar. So let me talk a little about that.

You know by this time that although I do listen I do see I do hear I do feel that I do talk.

English grammar is interesting because it is so simple. Once you really know how to diagram a sentence really know it, you know practically all you have to know about English grammar. In short any child thirteen years old properly taught can by that time have learned everything there is to learn about English grammar. So why make a fuss about it. However one does.

It is this that makes the English language such a vital language that the grammar of it is so simple and that one does make a fuss about it.

When I was up against the difficulty of putting down the complete conception that I had of an individual, the complete rhythm of a personality that I had gradually acquired by listening seeing feeling and experience, I was faced by the trouble that I had acquired all this knowledge gradually but when I had it I had it completely at one time. Now that may never have been a trouble to you but it was a terrible trouble to me. And a great deal of The Making of Americans was a struggle to do this thing, to make a whole present of something that it had taken a great deal of time to find out, but it was a whole there then within me and as such it had to be said.

That then and ever since has been a great deal of my work and it is that which has made me try so many ways to tell my story.

In The Making of Americans I tried it in a variety of ways. And my sentences grew longer and longer, my imaginary dependent clauses were constantly being dropped out, I struggled with relations between they them and then, I began with a relation between tenses that sometimes almost seemed to do it. And I went on and on and then one day after I had written

147

a thousand pages, this was in 1908 I just did not go on any more.

I did however immediately begin again. I began A Long Gay Book, that was going to be even longer than The Making of Americans and was going to be even more complicated, but then something happened in me and I said in Composition As Explanation, so then naturally it was natural that one thing an enormously long thing was not everything an enormously short thing was also not everything nor was it all of it a continuous present thing nor was it always and always beginning again.

And so this is The Making of Americans. A book one thousand pages long, and I worked over it three years, and I hope this makes it a little more understandable to you.

As I say I began A Long Gay Book and it was to be even longer than The Making of Americans and it was to describe not only every possible kind of a human being, but every possible kind of pairs of human beings and every possible threes and fours and fives of human beings and every possible kind of crowds of human beings. And I was going to do it as A Long Gay Book and at the same time I began several shorter books which were to illustrate the Long Gay Book, one called Many Many Women another Five, another Two and another G. M. P., Matisse Picasso and Gertrude Stein, but the chief book was to be the Long Gay Book and that was in a kind of way to go on and to keep going on and to go on before and it began in this way.

When they are very little just only a baby you can never tell which one is to be a lady.

There are some when they feel it inside them that it has been with them that there was once so very little of them, that they were a baby, help-less and no conscious feeling in them, that they knew nothing then when they were kissed and dandled and fixed by others who knew them when they could know nothing inside them or around them, some get from all this that once surely happened to them to that which was then every bit that was then them, there are some when they feel it later inside them that they were such once and that was all that there was then of them, there are some who have from such a knowing an uncertain curious kind of feeling in them that their having been so little once and knowing nothing makes it all a broken world for them that they have inside them, kills for them the everlasting feeling: and they spend their life in many ways, and always they are trying to make for themselves a new everlasting feeling.

One way perhaps of winning is to make a little one to come through them, little like the baby that once was all them and lost them their ever-lasting feeling. Some can win from just the feeling, the little one need not come, to give it to them.

And so always there is beginning and to some then a losing of the everlasting feeling. Then they make a baby to make for themselves a new beginning and so win for themselves a new everlasting feeling.

A LONG GAY BOOK (PLAIN EDITION)
RANDOM HOUSE, PAGE 13.

I knew while I was writing The Making of Americans that it was possible to describe every kind there is of men and women.

I began to wonder if it was possible to describe the way every possible kind of human being acted and felt in relation with any other kind of human being and I thought if this could be done it would make A Long Gay Book. It is naturally gayer describing what any one feels acts and does in relation to any other one than to describe what they just are what they are inside them.

And as I naturally found it livelier, I myself was becoming livelier just then. One does you know, when one has come to the conclusion that what is inside every one is not all there is of any one. I was, there is no doubt about it, I was coming to be livelier in relation to myself inside me and in relation to any one inside in them. This being livelier inside me kept on increasing and so you see it was a natural thing that as the Long Gay Book began, it did not go on. If it were to be really lively would it go on. Does one if one is really lively and I was really very lively then does one go on and does one if one is really very lively does one content oneself with describing what is going on inside in one and going on inside in every one in any one.

At any rate what happened is this and every one reading these things, A Long Gay Book, Many Many Women and G. M. P. will see, that it changed, it kept on changing, until at last it led to something entirely different something very short and lively to the Portrait of Mabel Dodge and the little book called Tender Buttons but all that I will talk about later. To go back to The Making of Americans and A Long Gay Book.

One must not forget that although life seems long it is very short, that although civilization seems long it is not so very long. If you think about how many generations, granting that your grandfather to you make a hundred years, if you think about that, it is extraordinary how very short is the history of the world in which we live, the world which is the world where there is a world for us. It is like the generations in the Bible, they really do not take so very long. Now when you are beginning realizing everything, this is a thing that is not confusing but is a thing that as you might say is at one time very long and at the same time not at all long. Twenty-five years roll around so quickly and in writing they can do one of two things, they can either roll around more or they can roll around less quickly.

In writing The Making of Americans they rolled around less quickly. In writing A Long Gay Book, they did not roll around at all, and therefore it did not go on it led to Tender Buttons and many other things. It may even have led to war but that is of no importance.

The Making of Americans rolled around very slowly, it was only three years but they rolled around slowly and that is inevitable when one conceives everything as being there inside in one. Of course everything is always inside in one, that anybody knows but the kind of a one that one is is all inside in one or it is partly not all inside in one. When one is beginning to know everything, and that happens as it does happen, you all know that, when one is beginning to know everything inside in one description strengthens it being all inside in one. That was for me the whole of The Making of Americans, it was the strengthening the prolonging of the existing of everything being inside in one. You may call that being younger you may not just as you feel about it but what is important about it is, that if everything is all inside in one then it takes longer to know it than when it is not so completely inside in one.

Therefore it takes longer to know everything when everything is all inside one than when it is not. Call it being young if you like, or call it not including anything that is not everything. It does not make any difference whether you are young or younger or older or very much older. That does not make any difference because after all as I say civilization is not very old if you think about it by hundreds of years and realize that your grandfather to you can very much more than make a hundred years if it happens right.

And so I say and I saw that a complete description of every kind of human being that ever could or would be living is not such a very extensive thing because after all it can be all contained inside in any one and finally it can be done.

So then in writing The Making of Americans it was to me an enormously long thing to do to describe every one and slowly it was not an enormously long thing to do to describe every one. Because after all as I say civilization is not a very long thing, twenty-five years roll around so quickly and four times twenty-five years make a hundred years and that makes a grandfather to a granddaughter. Everybody is interested when that happens to any one, because it makes it long and it makes it short. And so and this is the thing that made the change a necessary change from The Making of Americans to A Long Gay Book and then to Tender Buttons.

I will read you some few little things that will show this thing. A few things out of A Long Gay Book that show how it changed, changed from Making of Americans to Tender Buttons.

It is a simple thing to be quite certain that there are kinds in men and women. It is a simple thing and then not any one has any worrying to be doing about any one being any one. It is a simple thing to be quite certain that each one is one being a kind of them and in being that kind of a one is one being, doing, thinking, feeling, remembering and forgetting, loving, disliking, being angry, laughing, eating, drinking, talking, sleeping, waking like all of them of that kind of them. There are enough kinds in men and women so that any one can be interested in that thing that there are kinds in men and women.

A LONG GAY BOOK—PAGE 23.

Vrais says good good, excellent. Vrais listens and when he listens he says good good, excellent. Vrais listens and he being Vrais when he has listened he says good good, excellent.

Vrais listens, he being Vrais, he listens.

Anything is two things. Vrais was nicely faithful. He had been nicely faithful. Anything is two things.

He had been nicely faithful. In being one he was one who had he been one continuing would not have been one continuing being nicely faithful. He was one continuing, he was not continuing to be nicely faithful. In continuing he was being one being the one who was saying good

good, excellent but in continuing he was needing that he was believing that he was aspiring to be one continuing to be able to be saying good good, excellent. He had been one saying good good, excellent. He had been that one.

A LONG GAY BOOK—PAGE 53.

If the accumulation of inexpediency produces the withdrawing of the afternoon greeting then in the evening there is more preparation and this will take away the paper that has been lying where it could be seen. All the way that has the aging of a younger generation is part of the way that resembles anything that is not disappearing. It is not alright as colors are existing in being accommodating. They have a way that is identical.

A LONG GAY BOOK—PAGE 86.

Pardon the fretful autocrat who voices discontent. Pardon the colored water-color which is burnt. Pardon the intoning of the heavy way. Pardon the aristocrat who has not come to stay. Pardon the abuse which was begun. Pardon the yellow egg which has run. Pardon nothing yet, pardon what is wet, forget the opening now, and close the door again.

A LONG GAY BOOK—PAGE 100.

A private life is the long thick tree and the private life is the life for me. A tree which is thick is a tree which is thick. A life which is private is not what there is. All the times that come are the times I sing, all the singing I sing are the tunes I sing. I sing and I sing and the tunes I sing are what are tunes if they come and I sing. I sing I sing.

A LONG GAY BOOK—PAGE 107.

Suppose it did, suppose it did with a sheet and a shadow and a silver set of water, suppose it did.

A LONG GAY BOOK—PAGE 114.

When I was working with William James I completely learned one thing, that science is continuously busy with the complete description of something, with ultimately the complete description of anything with ultimately the complete description of everything. If this can really be done the complete description of everything then what else is there to do. We may well say nothing, but and this is the thing that makes everything continue to be anything, that after all what does happen is that as relatively few people spend all their time describing anything and they stop and so in the meantime as everything goes on somebody else can always commence and go on. And so description is really unending. When I began The Making of Americans I knew I really did know that a complete description was a possible thing, and certainly a complete description is a possible thing. But as it is a possible thing one can stop continuing to describe this everything. That is where philosophy comes in, it begins when one stops continuing describing everything.

And so this was the history of the writing of The Making of Americans and why I began A Long Gay Book. I said I would go on describing everything in A Long Gay Book, but as inevitably indeed really one does stop describing everything being at last really convinced that a description of everything is possible it was inevitable that I gradually stopped describing everything in A Long Gay Book.

Nevertheless it would be nice to really have described every kind there is of men and women, and it really would not be very hard to do but it would inevitably not be a Long Gay Book, but it would be a Making of Americans.

But I do not want to begin again or go on with what was begun because after all I know I really do know that it can be done and if it can be done why do it, particularly as I say one does know that civilization has after all not existed such a very long time if you count it by a hundred years, and each time there has been civilization it has not lasted such a long time if you count it by a hundred years, which makes a period that can connect you with some other one.

I hope you like what I say.

And so The Making of Americans has been done.

It must be remembered that whether they are China-men or Americans there are the same kinds in men and women and one can describe all the kinds of them. This I might have done.

And so then I began The Long Gay Book. As soon as I began the Long Gay Book I knew inevitably it would not go on to continue what The Making of Americans had begun. And why not. Because as my life was my life inside me but I was realizing begin-ning realizing that everything described would not do any more than tell all I knew about anything why should I tell all I knew about anything since after all I did know all I knew about anything.

So then I said I would begin again. I would not know what I knew about everything what I knew about anything.

And so the Long Gay Book little by little changed from a description of any one of any one and every-thing there was to be known about any one, to what if not was not not to be not known about any one about anything. And so it was necessary to let come what would happen to come because after all knowledge is what you know but what is happening is inevitably what is happening to come.

And so this brings us to other things.

In describing English literature I have explained that the twentieth century was the century not of sentences as was the eighteenth not of phrases as was the nineteenth but of paragraphs. And as I explained paragraphs were inevitable because as the nineteenth century came to its ending, phrases were no longer full of any meaning and the time had come when a whole thing was all there was of anything. Series immediately before and after made everybody clearly understand this thing. And so it was natural that in writing The Making of Americans I had proceeded to enlarge my paragraphs so as to include everything. What else could I do. In fact inevitably I made my sentences and my paragraphs do the same thing, made them be one and the same thing. This was inevitably because the nineteenth century having lived by phrases really had lost the feeling of sentences, and before this in English literature paragraphs had never been an end in themselves and now in the beginning of the twentieth century a whole thing, being what was assembled from its parts was a whole thing and so it was a paragraph. You will see that in The Making of Americans I did this thing, I made a paragraph so much a whole thing that it included in itself as a whole thing a whole sentence. That makes something clear to you does it not.

And this is what The Making of Americans was. Slowly it was not enough to satisfy myself with a whole thing as a paragraph as a whole thing and I will tell very much more about how that came about but The Making of Americans really carried it as far as it could be carried so I think the making a whole paragraph a whole thing.

Then at the same time is the question of time. The assembling of a thing to make a whole thing and each one of these whole things is one of a series, but beside this there is the important thing and the very American thing that everybody knows who is an American just how many seconds minutes or hours it is going to take to do a whole thing. It is singularly a sense for combination within a conception of the existence of a given space of time that makes the American thing the American thing, and the sense of this space of time must be within the whole thing as well as in the completed whole thing.

I felt this thing, I am an American and I felt this thing, and I made a continuous effort to create this thing in every paragraph that I made in The Making of Americans. And that is why after all this book is an American book an essentially American book, because this thing is an essentially American thing this sense of a space of time and what is to be done within this space of time not in any way excepting in the way that it is inevitable that there is this space of time and anybody who is an American feels what is inside this space of time and so well they do what they do within this space of time, and so ultimately it is a thing contained within. I wonder if I at all convey to you what I mean by this thing. I will try to tell it in every way I can as I have in all the writing that I have ever done. I am always trying to tell this thing that a space of time is a natural thing for an American to always have inside them as something in which they are continuously moving. Think of anything, of cowboys, of movies, of detective stories, of anybody who goes anywhere or stays at home and is an American and you will realize that it is something strictly American to conceive a space that is filled with moving, a space of time that is filled always filled with moving and my first real effort to express this thing which is an American thing began in writing The Making of Americans.

PORTRAITS
AND
REPETITION

IN Composition As Explanation I said nothing changes from generation to generation except the composition in which we live and the composition in which we live makes the art which we see and hear. I said in Lucy Church Amiably that women and children change, I said if men have not changed women and children have. But it really is of no importance even if this is true. The thing that is important is the way that portraits of men and women and children are written, by written I mean made. And by made I mean felt. Portraits of men and women and children are differently felt in every generation and by a generation one means any period of time. One does mean any period of time by a generation. A generation can be anywhere from two years to a hundred years. What was it somebody said that the only thing God could not do was to make a two year old mule in a minute. But the strange thing about the realization of existence is that like a train moving there is no real realization of it moving if it does not move against something and so that is what a generation does it shows that moving is existing. So then there are generations and in a way that too is not important because, and this thing is a thing to know, if and we in America have tried to make this thing a real thing, if the movement, that is any movement, is lively enough, perhaps it is possible to know that it is moving even if it is not moving against anything.

And so in a way the American way has been not to need that generations are existing. If this were really true and perhaps it is really true then really and truly there is a new way of making portraits of men and women and children. And I, I in my way have tried to do this thing.

It is true that generations are not of necessity existing that is to say if the actual movement within a thing is alive enough. A motor goes inside of an automobile and the car goes. In short this generation has conceived an intensity of movement so great that it has not to be seen against something else to be known, and therefore, this generation does not connect itself with anything, that is what makes this generation what it is and that is why it is American, and this is very important in connection with portraits of anything. I say portraits and not description and I will gradually explain why. Then also there is the important question of repetition and is there any such thing. Is there repetition or is there insistence. I am inclined to believe there is no such thing as repetition. And really how can there be. This is a thing about which I want you to think before I go on telling about portraits of anything. Think about all the detective stories everybody reads. The kind of crime is the same, and the idea of the story is very often the same, take for example a man like Wallace, he always has the same theme, take a man like Fletcher he always has the same theme, take any American ones, they too always have the scene, the same scene, the kind of invention that is necessary to make a general scheme is very limited in everybody's experience, every time one of the hundreds of times a newspaper man makes fun of my writing and of my repetition he always has the same theme, always having the same theme, that is, if you like, repetition, that is if you like the repeating that is the same thing, but once started expressing this thing, expressing any thing there can be no repetition because the essence of that expression is insistence, and if you insist you must each time use emphasis and if you use emphasis it is not possible while anybody is alive that they should use exactly the same emphasis. And so let us think seriously of the difference between repetition and insistence.

Anybody can be interested in a story of a crime because no matter how often the witnesses tell the same story the insistence is different. That is what makes life that the insistence is different, no matter how often you tell the same story if there is anything alive in the telling the emphasis is different. It has to be, anybody can know that.

It is very like a frog hopping he cannot ever hop exactly the same distance or the same way of hopping at every hop. A bird's singing is perhaps the nearest thing to repetition but if you listen they too vary their insistence. That is the human expression saying the same thing and in insisting and we all insist varying the emphasising.

I remember very well first beginning to be conscious of this thing. I became conscious of these things, I suppose anybody does when they first really know that the stars are worlds and that everything is moving, that is the first conscious feeling of necessary repetition, and it comes to one and it is very disconcerting. Then the second thing is when you first realize the history of various civilizations, that have been on this earth, that too makes one realize repetition and at the same time the difference of insistence. Each civilization insisted in its own way before it went away. I remember the first time I really realized this in this way was from reading a book we had at home of the excavations of Nineveh, but these emotions although they tell one so much and one really never forgets them, after all are not in one's daily living, they are like the books of Jules Verne terribly real terribly near but still not here. When I first really realized the inevitable repetition in human expression that was not repetition but insistence when I first began to be really conscious of it was when at about seventeen years of age, I left the more or less internal and solitary and concentrated life I led in California and came to Baltimore and lived with a lot of my relations and principally with a whole group of very lively little aunts who had to know anything.

If they had to know anything and anybody does they naturally had to say and hear it often, anybody does, and as there were ten and eleven of them they did have to say and hear said whatever was said and any one not hearing what it was they said had to come in to hear what had been said. That inevitably made everything said often. I began then to consciously listen to what anybody was saying and what they did say while they were saying what they were saying. This was not yet the beginning of writing but it was the beginning of knowing what there was that made there be no repetition. No matter how often what happened had happened any time any one told anything there was no repetition. This is what William James calls the Will to Live. If not nobody would live.

And so I began to find out then by listening the difference between repetition and insisting and it is a very important thing to know. You listen as you know.

Then there is another thing that also has something to do with repeating.

When all these eleven little aunts were listening as they were talking gradually some one of them was no longer listening. When this happened it might be that the time had come that any one or one of them was beginning repeating, that is was ceasing to be insisting or else perhaps it might be that the attention of one of some one of them had been worn out by adding something. What is the difference. Nothing makes any difference as long as some one is listening while they are talking.

That is what I gradually began to know.

Nothing makes any difference as long as some one is listening while they are talking. If the same person does the talking and the listening why so much the better there is just by so much the greater concentration. One may really indeed say that that is the essence of genius, of being most intensely alive, that is being one who is at the same time talking and listening. It is really that that makes one a genius. And it is necessary if you are to be really and truly alive it is necessary to be at once talking and listening, doing both things, not as if there were one thing, not as if they were two things, but doing them, well if you like, like the motor going inside and the car moving, they are part of the same thing.

I said in the beginning of saying this thing that if it were possible that a movement were lively enough it would exist so completely that it would not be necessary to see it moving against anything to know that it is moving. This is what we mean by life and in my way I have tried to make portraits of this thing always have tried always may try to make portraits of this thing.

If this existence is this thing is actually existing there can be no repetition. There is only repetition when there are descriptions being given of these things not when the things themselves are actually existing and this is therefore how my portrait writing began.

So we have now, a movement lively enough to be a thing in itself moving, it does not have to move against anything to know that it is moving, it does not need that there are generations existing.

Then we have insistence insistence that in its emphasis can never be repeating, because insistence is always alive and if it is alive it is never saying anything in the same way because emphasis can never be the same not even when it is most the same that is when it has been taught.

How do you like what you have.

This is a question that anybody can ask anybody. Ask it.

In asking it I began to make portraits of anybody.

How do you like what you have is one way of having an important thing to ask of any one.

That is essentially the portrait of any one, one portrait of any one.

I began to think about portraits of any one.

If they are themselves inside them what are they and what has it to do with what they do.

And does it make any difference what they do or how they do it, does it make any difference what they say or how they say it. Must they be in relation with any one or with anything in order to be one of whom one can make a portrait. I began to think a great deal about all these things.

Anybody can be interested in what anybody does but does that make any difference, is it all important.

Anybody can be interested in what anybody says, but does that make any difference, is it at all important.

I began to wonder about all that.

I began to wonder what it was that I wanted to have as a portrait, what there is that was to be the portrait.

I do not wonder so much now about that. I do not wonder about that at all any more. Now I wonder about other things, I wonder if what has been done makes any difference.

I wonder now if it is necessary to stand still to live if it is not necessary to stand still to live, and if it is if that is not perhaps to be a new way to write a novel. I wonder if you know what I mean. I do not quite know whether I do myself. I will not know until I have written that novel.

I have just tried to begin in writing Four In America because I am certain that what makes American success is American failure.

I am certain about that.

Some time I will explain that at great length but now I want to tell about how I wrote portraits. I wrote portraits knowing that each one is themselves inside them and something about them perhaps everything about them will tell some one all about that thing all about what is themselves inside them and I was then hoping completely hoping that I was that one the one who would tell that thing. Perhaps I was that one.

There is another thing that one has to think about, that is about thinking clearly and about confusion. That is something about which I have almost as much to say as I have about anything.

The difference between thinking clearly and confusion is the same difference that there is between repetition and insistence. A great many think that they know repetition when they see or hear it but do they. A great many think that they know confusion when they know or see it or hear it, but do they. A thing that seems very clear, seems very clear but is it. A thing that seems to be exactly the same thing may seem to be a repetition but is it. All this can be very exciting, and it had a great deal to do with portrait writing.

As I say a thing that is very clear may easily not be clear at all, a thing that may be confused may be very clear. But everybody knows that. Yes anybody knows that. It is like the necessity of knowing one's father and one's mother one's grandmothers and one's grandfathers, but is it necessary and if it is can it be no less easily forgotten.

As I say the American thing is the vitality of movement, so that there need be nothing against which the movement shows as movement. And if this vitality is lively enough is there in that clarity any confusion is there in that clarity any repetition. I myself do not think so. But I am inclined to believe that there is really no difference between clarity and confusion, just think of any life that is alive, is there really any difference between clarity and confusion. Now I am quite certain that there is really if anything is alive no difference between clarity and confusion. When I first began writing portraits of any one I was not so sure, not so certain of this thing that there is no difference between clarity and confusion. I was however almost certain then when I began writing portraits that if anything is alive there is no such thing as repetition. I do not know that I have ever changed my mind about that. At any rate I did then begin the writing of portraits and I will tell you now all there is to tell about all that. I had of course written about every kind of men and women in The Making of Americans but in writing portraits I wanted not to write about any one doing or even saying anything, I found this a difficult enough thing to begin.

I remember very well what happened. As I say I had the habit of conceiving myself as completely talking and listening, listening was talking and talking was listening and in so doing I conceived what I at that time called the rhythm of anybody's personality. If listening was talking and talking was listening then and at the same time any little movement any little expression was a resemblance, and a resemblance was something that presupposed remembering.

Listening and talking did not presuppose resemblance and as they do not presuppose resemblance, they do not necessitate remembering. Already then as you see there was a complication which was a bother to me in my conception of the rhythm of a personality. I have for so many years tried to get the better of that the better of this bother. The bother was simply that and one may say it is the bother that has always been a bother to anybody for anybody conceiving anything. Dillinger is dead it was even a bother for him.

As I say as I felt the existence of anybody later as I felt the existence of anybody or anything, there was then the listening and talking which I was doing which anybody was doing and there were the little things that made of any one some one resembling some one.

Any one does of course by any little thing by any little way by any little expression, any one does of course resemble some one, and any one can notice this thing notice this resemblance and in so doing they have to remember some one and this is a different thing from listening and talking. In other words the making of a portrait of any one is as they are existing and as they are existing has nothing to do with remembering any one or anything. Do you see my point, but of course yes you do. You do see that there are two things and not one and if one wants to make one portrait of some one and not two you can see that one can be bothered completely bothered by this thing. As I say it is something that has always bothered any one.

Funnily enough the cinema has offered a solution of this thing. By a continuously moving picture of any one there is no memory of any other thing and there is that thing existing, it is in a way if you like one portrait of anything not a number of them. There again you do see what I mean.

Now I in my way wanted to make portraits of any one later in Tender Buttons I also wanted to make portraits of anything as one thing as one portrait and although and that was my trouble in the beginning I felt the thing the person as existing and as everything in that person entered in to make that person little ways and expressions that made resembling, it was necessary for me nevertheless not to realize these things as remembering but to realize the one thing as existing and there they were and I was noticing, well you do see that it was a bother and I was bothering very much bothering about this thing.

In the beginning and I will read you some portraits to show you this I continued to do what I was doing in the Making of Americans, I was doing what the cinema was doing, I was making a continuous succession of the statement of what that person was until I had not many things but one thing. As I read you some of the portraits of that period you will see what I mean.

I of course did not think of it in terms of the cinema, in fact I doubt whether at that time I had ever seen a cinema but, and I cannot repeat this too often any one is of one's period and this our period was undoubtedly the period of the cinema and series production. And each of us in our own way are bound to express what the world in which we are living is doing.

You see then what I was doing in my beginning portrait writing and you also understand what I mean when I say there was no repetition. In a cinema picture no two pictures are exactly alike each one is just that much different from the one before, and so in those early portraits there was as I am sure you will realize as I read them to you also as there was in The Making of Americans no repetition. Each time that I said the somebody whose portrait I was writing was something that something was just that much different from what I had just said that somebody was and little by little in this way a whole portrait came into being, a portrait that was not description and that was made by each time, and I did a great many times, say it, that somebody was something, each time there was a difference just a difference enough so that it could go on and be a present something. Oh yes you all do understand. You understand this. You see that in order to do this there must be no remembering, remembering is repetition, remembering is also confusion. And this too you will presently know all about.

Remembering is repetition anybody can know that. In doing a portrait of any one, the repetition consists in knowing that that one is a kind of a one, that the things he does have been done by others like him that the things he says have been said by others like him, but, and this is the important thing, there is no repetition in hearing and saying the things he hears and says when he is hearing and saying them. And so in doing a portrait of him if it were possible to make that portrait a portrait of him saying and hearing what he says and hears while he is saying and hearing it there is then in so doing neither memory nor repetition no matter how often that which he says and hears is heard and said. This was the discovery I made as I talked and listened more and more and this is what I did when I made portraits of every one I know. I said what I knew as they said and heard what they heard and said until I had completely emptied myself of all they were that is all that they were in being one hearing and saying what they heard and said in every way that they heard and said anything.

And this is the reason why that what I wrote was exciting although those that did not really see what it was thought it was repetition. If it had been repetition it would not have been exciting but it was exciting and it was not repetition. It never is. I never repeat that is while I am writing.

As I say what one repeats is the scene in which one is acting, the days in which one is living, the coming and going which one is doing, anything one is remembering is a repetition, but existing as a human being, that is being listening and hearing is never repetition. It is not repetition if it is that which you are actually doing because naturally each time the emphasis is different just as the cinema has each time a slightly different thing to make it all be moving. And each one of us has to do that, otherwise there is no existing. As Galileo remarked, it does move.

So you see what I mean about those early portraits and the middle part of The Making of Americans. I built them up little by little each time I said it it changed just a little and then when I was completely emptied of knowing that the one of whom I was making a portrait existed I had made a portrait of that one.

To go back to something I said that remembering was the only repetition, also that remembering was the only confusion. And I think you begin to see what I mean by that.

No matter how complicated anything is, if it is not mixed up with remembering there is no confusion, but and that is the trouble with a great many so called intelligent people they mix up remembering with talking and listening, and as a result they have theories about anything but as remembering is repetition and confusion, and being existing that is listening and talking is action and not repetition intelligent people although they talk as if they knew something are really confusing, because they are so to speak keeping two times going at once, the repetition time of remembering and the actual time of talking but, and as they are rarely talking and listening, that is the talking being listening and the listening being talking, although they are clearly saying something they are not clearly creating something, because they are because they always are remembering, they are not at the same time talking and listening. Do you understand. Do you any or all of you understand. Anyway that is the way it is. And you hear it even if you do not say it in the way I say it as I hear it and say it.

I say I never repeat while I am writing because while I am writing I am most completely, and that is if you like being a genius, I am most entirely and completely listening and talking, the two in one and the one in two and that is having completely its own time and it has in it no element of remembering. Therefore there is in it no element of confusion, therefore there is in it no element of repetition. Do you do you do you really understand.

And does it make any difference to you if you do

understand. It makes an awful lot of difference to me. It is very exciting to have all this be.

Gradually then I began making portraits. And how did I begin.

When I first began writing although I felt very strongly that something that made that some one be some one was something that I must use as being them, I naturally began to describe them as they were doing anything. In short I wrote a story as a story, that is the way I began, and slowly I realized this confusion, a real confusion, that in writing a story one had to be remembering, and that novels are soothing because so many people one may say everybody can remember almost anything. It is this element of remembering that makes novels so soothing. But and that was the thing that I was gradually finding out listening and talking at the same time that is realizing the existence of living being actually existing did not have in it any element of remembering and so the time of existing was not the same as in the novels that were soothing. As I say all novels are soothing because they make anything happen as they can happen that is by remembering anything. But and I kept wondering as I talked and listened all at once, I wondered is there any way of making what I know come out as I know it, come out not as remembering. I found this very exciting. And I began to make portraits.

I kept on knowing people by resemblances, that

was partly memory and it bothered me but I knew I had to do everything and I tried to do that so completely that I would lose it. I made charts and charts of everybody who looked like anybody until I got so that I hardly knew which one I knew on the street and which one looked like them. I did this until at last any one looking like any one else had no importance. It was not a thing that was any longer an important thing, I knew completely how any one looked like any other one and that became then only a practical matter, a thing one might know as what any one was liable to do, but this to me then was no longer interesting. And so I went on with portrait writing.

I cannot tell you although I think I can, that, as I can read any number of soothing novels in fact nothing else soothes me I found it not a thing that it was interesting to do. And I think now you know why it was not an interesting thing to do. We in this period have not lived in remembering, we have living in moving being necessarily so intense that existing is indeed something, is indeed that thing that we are doing. And so what does it really matter what anybody does. The newspapers are full of what anybody does and anybody knows what anybody does but the thing that is important is the intensity of anybody's existence. Once more I remind you of Dillinger. It was not what he did that was exciting but the excitement of what he was as being exciting that was exciting. There is a world of difference and in it there is essentially no remembering.

And so I am trying to tell you what doing portraits meant to me, I had to find out what it was inside any one, and by any one I mean every one I had to find out inside every one what was in them that was intrinsically exciting and I had to find out not by what they said not by what they did not by how much or how little they resembled any other one but I had to find it out by the intensity of movement that there was inside in any one of them. And of course do not forget, of course I was interested in any one. I am. Of course I am interested in any one. And in any one I must or else I must betake myself to some entirely different occupation and I do not think I will, I must find out what is moving inside them that makes them them, and I must find out how I by the thing moving excitedly inside in me can make a portrait of them.

You can understand why I did it so often, why I did it in so many ways why I say that there is no repetition because, and this is absolutely true, that the exciting thing inside in any one if it is really inside in them is not a remembered thing, if it is really inside in them, it is not a confused thing, it is not a repeated thing. And if I could in any way and I have done it in every way if I could make a portrait of that inside them without any description of what they are doing and what they are saying then I too was neither repeating, nor remembering nor being in a confusion.

You see what I mean by what I say. But I know you do.

Will you see it as clearly when I read you some of the portraits that I have written. Maybe you will but I doubt it. But if you do well then if you do you will see what I have done and do do.

A thing you all know is that in the three novels written in this generation that are the important things written in this generation, there is, in none of them a story. There is none in Proust in The Making of Americans or in Ulysses. And this is what you are now to begin to realize in this description I am giving you of making portraits.

It is of course perfectly natural that autobiographies are being well written and well read. You do see anybody can see that so much happens every day and that anybody literally anybody can read or hear about it told the day that it happens. A great deal happens every day and any day and as I say anybody literally anybody can hear or read everything or anything about anything or everything that happens every day just as it has happened or is happening on that day. You do see what that means. Novels then which tell a story are really then more of the same much more of the same, and of course anybody likes more of the same and so a great many novels are written and a great many novels are read telling more of these stories but you can see you do see that the important things written in this generation do not tell a story. You can see that it is natural enough.

You begin definitely to feel that it had to be that I was to write portraits as I wrote them. I began to write them when I was about in the middle of The Making of Americans, and if you read The Making of Americans you will realize why this was inevitable.

I began writing the portraits of any one by saying what I knew of that one as I talked and listened that one, and each time that I talked and listened that one I said what I knew they were then. This made my early portraits and some that I finally did such as Four Dishonest Ones Told by a Description of What They Do, Matisse and Picasso and a lot of others, did as completely as I then could strictly did this thing. Every time I said what they were I said it so that they were this thing, and each time I said what they were as they were, as I was, naturally more or less but never the same thing each time that I said what they were I said what they were, not that they were different nor that I was different but as it was not the same moment which I said I said it with a difference. So finally I was emptied of saying this thing, and so no longer said what they were.

FOUR DISHONEST ONES.

Told By a Description Of What They Do.

They are what they are. They have not been changing. They are what they are.

Each one is what that one is. Each is what each is. They are not needing to be changing.

One is what she is. She does not need to be changing. She is what she is. She is not changing. She is what she is.

She is not changing. She is knowing nothing of not changing. She is not needing to be changing.

What is she doing. She is working. She is not needing to be changing. She is working very well, she is not needing to be changing. She has been working very hard. She has been suffering. She is not needing to be changing.

She has been living and working, she has been quiet and working, she has been suffering and working, she has been watching and working, she has been waiting, she has been working, she has been waiting and working, she is not needing to be changing.

PORTRAITS AND PRAYERS, PAGE 57.

At this time also I wanted to make portraits of places, I did. I did make them of the Bon Marché, of the Galeries Lafayette, of a crowd at Mi-Careme, I have always liked what I did with that one. It was completely something. And there again in doing the portraits of these places and these crowds, I did Italians, and Americans too like that, I continued to do as I had done in The Making of Americans. I told exactly and completely each time of telling what that one is inside in them. As I told you in comparing it to a cinema picture one second was never the same as the second before or after.

MI-CAREME

There was a man who said one could recognize him when one saw him again by the scar on the end of his nose and under his eye but these scars were very little ones almost not anything and one would remember him because he was one who had been saying that he was a man tired of working tired of being one being working, and that he would be very amusing, he could be amusing by saying something that would make any one listening begin blushing but, he said, he would not do such a thing he would be politely amusing and he was amusing and some being amused by him were not frightened by him. He might have been amusing to some who were at the same time ones frightened by him. He might be very amusing to some who would never in any way think that he could frighten any one.

PORTRAITS AND PRAYERS, PAGE 173.

At any rate I did these portraits and they were very

exciting, they were exciting to me and they were exciting to others who read them.

Then slowly once more I got bothered, after all I listened and talked but that was not all I did in knowing at any present time when I was stating anything what anything was. I was also looking, and that could not be entirely left out.

The trouble with including looking, as I have already told you, was that in regard to human beings looking inevitably carried in its train realizing movements and expression and as such forced me into recognizing resemblances, and so forced remembering and in forcing remembering caused confusion of present with past and future time.

Do you see what I mean. But certainly you certainly do. And so I began again to do portraits but this time it was not portraits of men and women and children, it was portraits of anything and so I made portraits of rooms and food and everything because there I could avoid this difficulty of suggesting remembering more easily while including looking with listening and talking than if I were to describe human beings. I will go a little more into that.

This is the great difficulty that bothered anybody creating anything in this generation. The painters naturally were looking, that was their occupation and they had too to be certain that looking was not confusing itself with remembering. Remembering with them takes the form of suggesting in their painting in place of having actually created the thing in itself that they are painting.

In writing the thing that is the difficulty is the question of confusing time, and this is the thing that bothered and still bothers any one in this generation. Later on in another writing I will tell about how this thing that is time has to do with grammar vocabulary and tenses. But now I am keeping strictly to the matter of portraits and repetition.

I began to make portraits of things and enclosures that is rooms and places because I needed to completely face the difficulty of how to include what is seen with hearing and listening and at first if I were to include a complicated listening and talking it would be too difficult to do. That is why painters paint still lives. You do see why they do.

So I began to do this thing, I tried to include color and movement and what I did is what you have all either read or heard of, a volume called Tender Buttons.

I for a time did not make portraits because as I was trying to live in looking, and looking was not to mix itself up with remembering I wished to reduce to its minimum listening and talking. In Tender Buttons, I described anything, and I will read you a few things to show you what I did then.

A DOG.

A little monkey goes like a donkey that means
to say that means to say that more sighs last goes.
Leave with it. A little monkey goes like a donkey.

TENDER BUTTONS, PAGE 26.

Cloudiness what is cloudiness, is it a lining, is
it a roll, is it melting.

TENDER BUTTONS, PAGE 38.

A hurt mended stick, a hurt mended cup, a hurt
mended article of exceptional relaxation and
annoyance, a hurt mended, hurt and mended is
so necessary that no mistake is intended.

TENDER BUTTONS, PAGE 43.

Abandon a garden and the house is bigger.
This is not smiling. This is comfortable. There is
the comforting of predilection. An open object
is establishing the loss that there was when the
vase was not inside the place. It was not wander-
ing.

PORTRAITS AND PRAYERS, PAGE 101.

You see what I mean, I did express what something
was, a little by talking and listening to that thing, but
a great deal by looking at that thing.

This as I say has been the great problem of our
generation, so much happens and anybody at any
moment knows everything that is happening that
things happening although interesting are not really

exciting. And an artist an artist inevitably has to do what is really exciting. That is what he is inside him, that is what an artist really is inside him, he is exciting, and if he is not there is nothing to any of it.

And so the excitement in me was then that I was to more and more include looking to make it a part of listening and talking and I did the portrait of Mabel Dodge and Susie Assado and Preciocilla and some others. But this was all after I had done Tender Buttons.

I began to wonder at at about this time just what one saw when one looked at anything really looked at anything. Did one see sound, and what was the relation between color and sound, did it make itself by description by a word that meant it or did it make itself by a word in itself. All this time I was of course not interested in emotion or that anything happened. I was less interested then in these things than I ever had been. I lived my life with emotion and with things happening but I was creating in my writing by simply looking. I was as I say at that time reducing as far as it was possible for me to reduce them, talking and listening.

I became more and more excited about how words which were the words that made whatever I looked at look like itself were not the words that had in them any quality of description. This excited me very much at that time.

And the thing that excited me so very much at that

time and still does is that the words or words that make what I looked at be itself were always words that to me very exactly related themselves to that thing the thing at which I was looking, but as often as not had as I say nothing whatever to do with what any words would do that described that thing.

Those of you that have seen Four Saints in Three Acts must know do know something of what I mean.

Of course by the time Four Saints was written I had mastered very much what I was doing then when I wrote Tender Buttons. By the time I wrote the Four Saints I had written a great a great many portraits and I had in hundreds of ways related words, then sentences then paragraphs to the thing at which I was looking and I had also come to have happening at the same time looking and listening and talking without any bother about resemblances and remembering.

One of the things as I said that made me most anxious at one time was the relation of color to the words that exactly meant that but had no element in it of description. One portrait I did I will read it to you of Lipschitz did this color thing better than I had ever before been able to do it.

LIPSCHITZ

Like and like likely and likely likely and likely like and like.

He had a dream. He dreamed he heard a pheasant calling and very likely a pheasant was calling.

To whom went.

He had a dream he dreamed he heard a pheasant calling and most likely a pheasant was calling.

In time.

PORTRAITS AND PRAYERS, PAGE 63.

Thus for over a very considerable period of time sometimes a great many at a time and sometimes one at a time and sometimes several at a time I continued to do portraits. Around about this time I did a second one of Carl Van Vechten, one of Sherwood Anderson, one of Cocteau and a second one of Picasso. They were different from those that I had done in the beginning and very different from those I did just after doing Tender Buttons. These were less concentrated, they moved more although the movement was definitely connected with color and not so closely connected with talking and listening.

VAN OR TWENTY YEARS AFTER

A SECOND PORTRAIT OF CARL VAN VECHTEN.

Twenty years after, as much as twenty years after in as much as twenty years after, after twenty years and so on. It is it is it is it is.

Keep it in sight all right.

Not to the future but to the fuchsia.

Tied and untied and that is all there is about
it. And as tied and as beside, and as beside and
tied. Tied and untied and beside and as beside
and as untied and as tied and as untied and as
beside.

PORTRAITS AND PRAYERS, PAGE 157.

And then slowly it changed again, talking and listening came slowly again to be more important than
that at which I was looking. Talking and listening
became more important again but at the same time
that it was talking and listening it had within itself
an entirely different emotion of moving.

Let me tell you just what I did as I did this thing.

As always happens one commences again. However
often it happens one does commence again and now in
my way I did commence again.

I was again bothered about something and it had
to do as my bother always has had to do with a thing
being contained within itself.

I realized that granted looking and listening and
talking being all happening at one time and that I had
been finding the words that did create that thing did
create the portrait that was the object of the looking
listening and talking I had been doing nevertheless I
had been losing something, something I had had, in
The Making of Americans and in Tender Buttons,
that is a thing contained within itself.

As I say a motor goes inside and the car goes on,

194

but my business my ultimate business as an artist was not with where the car goes as it goes but with the movement inside that is of the essence of its going. And had I in these rather beautiful portraits I had been writing had I a little lost this thing. Whether I had or whether I had not began a little to worry me not really worry but to be there inside me, had I lost a little the excitement of having this inside me. Had I. I did not think I really had but had I.

This brings me back once more to the subject of repetition.

The composition we live in changes but essentially what happens does not change. We inside us do not change but our emphasis and the moment in which we live changes. That is it is never the same moment it is never the same emphasis at any successive moment of existing. Then really what is repetition. It is very interesting to ask and it is a very interesting thing to know.

If you think anything over and over and eventually in connection with it you going to succeed or fail, succeeding and failing is repetition because you are always either succeeding or failing but any two moments of thinking it over is not repetition. Now you see that is where I differ from a great many people who say I repeat and they do not. They do not think their succeeding or failing is what makes repetition, in other words they do not think that what happens makes repetition but that it is the moment to moment emphasizing that makes repetition. Now I think the succeeding and failing is what makes the repetition not the moment to moment emphasizing that makes repetition.

Instinctively as I say you all agree with me because really in these days you all like crime stories or have liked crime stories or if you have not you should have and at any rate you do like newspapers or radio or funny papers, and in all these it is the moment to moment emphasis in what is happening that is interesting, the succeeding and failing is really not the thing that is interesting.

In the portraits that I did in that period of which I have just been speaking the later period considerably after the war the strictness of not letting remembering mix itself with looking and listening and talking which began with The Making of Americans and went on all through Tender Buttons and what came immediately after, all the period of Geography and Plays this strictness perhaps weakened a little weakened a little because and that in a way was an astonishment to me, I found that I was for a little while very much taken with the beauty of the sounds as they came from me as I made them.

This is a thing that may be at any time a temptation. This temptation came to me a little after the Saint Remy period when I wrote Saints in Seven, Four Religions, Capital Capitals. The strict discipline that I had given myself, the absolute refusal of never

196

using a word that was not an exact word all through the Tender Buttons and what I may call the early Spanish and Geography and Play period finally resulted in things like Susie Assado and Preciocilla etc. in an extraordinary melody of words and a melody of excitement in knowing that I had done this thing.

Then in concentrating this melody I wrote in Saint Remy these things I have just mentioned Four Religions, Capital Capitals, Saints in Seven and a great many other things. In doing these I concentrated the internal melody of existence that I had learned in relation to things seen into the feeling I then had there in Saint Remy of light and air and air moving and being still. I worked at these things then with a great deal of concentration and as it was to me an entirely new way of doing it I had as a result a very greatly increased melody. This melody for a little while after rather got the better of me and it was at that time that I wrote these portraits of which I have just spoken, the second Picasso, the second Carl Van Vechten, the Jean Cocteau, Lipschitz, the Sitwells, Edith Sitwell, Joe Davidson, quantities of portraits. Portraits after my concentrated effort at Saint Remy to really completely and exactly find the word for the air and sky and light and existence down there was relatively a simple thing and I as you may say held these portraits in my hand and they came easily and beautifully and truly. But as I say I did begin to think that I was rather drunk with what I had done. And I am always one to prefer being sober. I must be sober. It is so much more exciting to be sober, to be exact and concentrated and sober. So then as I say I began again.

So here we have it. There was the period of The Making of Americans portraiture, when by listening and talking I conceived at every moment the existence of some one, and I put down each moment that I had the existence of that one inside in me until I had completely emptied myself of this that I had had as a portrait of that one. This as I say made what has been called repetition but, and you will see, each sentence is just the difference in emphasis that inevitably exists in the successive moment of my containing within me the existence of that other one achieved by talking and listening inside in me and inside in that one. These were the early portraits I did. Then this slowly changed to portraits of spaces inclosed with or without somebody in them but written in the same way in the successive moments of my realizing them. As I said it was if you like, it was like a cinema picture made up of succession and each moment having its own emphasis that is its own difference and so there was the moving and the existence of each moment as it was in me.

Then as I said I had the feeling that something should be included and that something was looking, and so concentrating on looking I did the Tender

Buttons because it was easier to do objects than people if you were just looking. Then I began to do plays to make the looking have in it an element of moving and during this time I also did portraits that did the same thing. In doing these things I found that I created a melody of words that filled me with a melody that gradually made me do portraits easily by feeling the melody of any one. And this then began to bother me because perhaps I was getting drunk with melody and I do not like to be drunk I like to be sober and so I began again.

I began again not to let the looking be predominating not to have the listening and talking be predominating but to once more denude all this of anything in order to get back to the essence of the thing contained within itself. That led me to some very different writing that I am going to tell about in the next thing I write but it also led to some portraits that I do think did do what I was then hoping would be done that is at least by me, would be done in this way if it were to be done by me.

Of these there were quite a number but perhaps two that did it the most completely the thing I wanted to do were portraits of George Hugnet and Bernard Fay. I will read them to you and you will see what I mean. All the looking was there the talking and listening was there but instead of giving what I was realizing at any and every moment of them and of me until I was empty of them I made them contained within the thing I wrote that was them. The thing in itself folded itself up inside itself like you might fold a thing up to be another thing which is that thing inside in that thing.

Do you see what I mean.

If you think how you fold things or make a boat or anything else out of paper or getting anything to be inside anything, the hole in the doughnut or the apple in the dumpling perhaps you will see what I mean. I will try and tell a little more about this thing and how I felt about this thing and how it happened.

This time I do repeat; in going over this again, there was the portrait writing of The Making of Americans period. There was the portrait writing of the Tender Buttons period, Mabel Dodge came into that. There was the portrait writing of the Geography and Plays period, which ended up with Capital Capitals, and then there was the portrait writing of the Useful Knowledge period, including portraits of Sherwood Anderson and Carl Van Vechten. Of course in each one of these periods there were many many portraits written as I wrote portraits of almost any one and as at all times I write practically every day, to be sure not long but practically every day and if you write not long but practically every day you do get a great deal written. This is what I do and so I do do get a great deal written. I have written a great many portraits.

So then as I said at the end of all this I had come to

know I had a melody and to be certain of my melody that melody carried me to be sure always by looking and listening and talking but melody did carry me and so as always I had once more to begin again and I began again.

Melody should always be a by-product it should never be an end in itself it should not be a thing by which you live if you really and truly are one who is to do anything and so as I say I very exactly began again.

I had begun again some time before in working at grammar and sentences and paragraphs and what they mean and at plays and how they disperse themselves in relation to anything seen. And soon I was so completely concerned with these things that melody, beauty if you like was once more as it should always be a by-product.

I did at the same time as I did plays and grammar at this time, I did do portraits in these portraits I felt an entirely different thing. How could a thing if it is a human being if it is anything be entirely contained within itself. Of course it is, but is it and how is it and how did I know that it is.

This was the thing that I found then to be completely interesting, this was the thing I found then to be completely exciting. How was anything contained within itself.

I felt that I began then to feel any one to be inside them very differently than I had ever found any one be themselves inside them. This was the time that I wrote Lucy Church Amiably which quite definitely as a conception of what is seen was contained by itself inside it, although there it was a conceiving of what I was looking at as a landscape was to be itself inside in it, it was I said to be like an engraving and I think it is. But the people in it were in it as contained within the whole of it. I wanted however to do portraits where there was more movement inside in the portrait and yet it was to be the whole portrait completely held within that inside.

I began to feel movement to be a different thing than I had felt it to be.

It was to me beginning to be a less detailed thing and at the same time a thing that existed so completely inside in it and it was it was so completely inside that really looking and listening and talking were not a way any longer needed for me to know about this thing about movement being existing.

And how could I have this happen, let me read you the short portrait of George Hugnet and perhaps you will see what I mean. It is all there.

It really does not make any difference who George Hugnet was or what he did or what I said, all that was necessary was that there was something completely contained within itself and being contained within itself was moving, not moving in relation to anything not moving in relation to itself but just moving, I think I almost at that time did this thing. Do you at all in this portrait of George Hugnet that I will now read to you do you really see what I mean and in this portrait of Bernard Fay.

GEORGE HUGNET

George Genevieve Geronimo straightened it out without their finding it out.

Grammar makes George in our ring which Grammar makes George in our ring.

Grammar is as disappointed not is as grammar is as disappointed.

Grammar is not as Grammar is as disappointed.

George is in our ring. Grammar is not is disappointed. In are ring.

George Genevieve in are ring.

PORTRAITS AND PRAYERS, PAGE 66.

BERNARD FAY

Patience is amiable and amiably.

What is amiable and amiably.

Patience is amiable and amiably.

What is impatience.

Impatience is amiable and amiably.

PORTRAITS AND PRAYERS, PAGE 42.

Anyway this was to me a tremendously important thing and why. Well it was an important thing in itself for me but it was also an important thing because it made me realize what poetry really is.

This has something to do with what Edgar Allan Poe is.

But now to make you understand, that although I was as usual looking listening and talking perhaps more than ever at that time and leading a very complicated and perhaps too exciting every day living, never the less it really did not matter what I saw or said or heard, or if you like felt, because now there was at last something that was more vibrant than any of all that and somehow some way I had isolated it and in a way had gotten it written. It was about that time that I wrote Four Saints.

This was all very exciting and it went on and I did not do a great many portraits at that time. I wrote a great deal of poetry a great many plays and operas and some novels in which I tried again to do this thing, in one or two I more or less did, one called Brim Beauvais, I very often did, that is I created something out of something without adding anything, do you see what I mean.

It does mean something I do assure you it does mean something although it is very difficult to say it in any way except in the way that I said it then.

And so as I say I did not write a great many portraits at that time.

Then slowly I got a little tired, all that had been tremendously exciting, and one day then I began to write the Autobiography of Alice B. Toklas. You all know the joke of that, and in doing it I did an entirely different something something that I had been thinking about for some time and that had come out of some poetry I had been writing, Before The Flowers Of Friendship Faded Friendship Faded, but that is too long a story to begin now but it will be all told in Poetry and Grammar.

However the important thing was that for the first time in writing, I felt something outside me while I was writing, hitherto I had always had nothing but what was inside me while I was writing. Beside that I had been going for the first time since my college days to lectures. I had been going to hear Bernard Fay lecture about Franco-American things and I had become interested in the relation of a lecturer to his audience. I had never thought about an audience before not even when I wrote Composition As Explanation which was a lecture but now I suddenly began, to feel the outside inside and the inside outside and it was perhaps not so exciting but it was very interesting. Anyway it was quite exciting.

And so I wrote the Autobiography of Alice B. Toklas and told what happened as it had happened.

As I said way back, as now everybody at any moment can know what it is that happens while it happens, what happens is interesting but it is not really exciting. And I am not sure that I am not right about that. I hope you all think I am right about that. At any rate it is true there is something much more exciting than anything that happens and now and always I am writing the portrait of that.

I have been writing the portraits of Four In America, trying to write Grant, and Wilbur Wright and Henry James and Washington do other things than they did do so as to try to find out just what it is that what happens has to do with what is.

I have finished that and now I am trying in these lectures to tell what is by telling about how it happened that I told about what it is.

I hope you quite all see what I mean. Anyway I suppose inevitably I will go on doing it.

POETRY
AND
GRAMMAR

W HAT is poetry and if you know what poetry is what is prose.

There is no use in telling more than you know, no not even if you do not know it.

But do you do you know what prose is and do you know what poetry is.

I have said that the words in plays written in poetry are more lively than the same words written by the same poet in other kinds of poetry. It undoubtedly was true of Shakespeare, is it inevitably true of everybody. That is one thing to think about. I said that the words in a play written in prose are not as lively words as the words written in other prose by the same writer. This is true of Goldsmith and I imagine it is true of almost any writer.

There again there is something to know.

One of the things that is a very interesting thing to know is how you are feeling inside you to the words that are coming out to be outside of you.

Do you always have the same kind of feeling in relation to the sounds as the words come out of you or do you not. All this has so much to do with grammar and with poetry and with prose.

Words have to do everything in poetry and prose and some writers write more in articles and prepositions and some say you should write in nouns, and of course one has to think of everything.

A noun is a name of anything, why after a thing is

named write about it. A name is adequate or it is not. If it is adequate then why go on calling it, if it is not then calling it by its name does no good.

People if you like to believe it can be made by their names. Call anybody Paul and they get to be a Paul call anybody Alice and they get to be an Alice perhaps yes perhaps no, there is something in that, but generally speaking, things once they are named the name does not go on doing anything to them and so why write in nouns. Nouns are the name of anything and just naming names is alright when you want to call a roll but is it any good for anything else. To be sure in many places in Europe as in America they do like to call rolls.

As I say a noun is a name of a thing, and therefore slowly if you feel what is inside that thing you do not call it by the name by which it is known. Everybody knows that by the way they do when they are in love and a writer should always have that intensity of emotion about whatever is the object about which he writes. And therefore and I say it again more and more one does not use nouns.

Now what other things are there beside nouns, there are a lot of other things beside nouns.

When you are at school and learn grammar grammar is very exciting. I really do not know that anything has ever been more exciting than diagraming sentences. I suppose other things may be more exciting to others when they are at school but to me undoubtedly when I was at school the really completely exciting thing was diagraming sentences and that has been to me ever since the one thing that has been completely exciting and completely completing. I like the feeling the everlasting feeling of sentences as they diagram themselves.

In that way one is completely possessing something and incidentally one's self. Now in that diagraming of the sentences of course there are articles and prepositions and as I say there are nouns but nouns as I say even by definition are completely not interesting, the same thing is true of adjectives. Adjectives are not really and truly interesting. In a way anybody can know always has known that, because after all adjectives effect nouns and as nouns are not really interesting the thing that effects a not too interesting thing is of necessity not interesting. In a way as I say anybody knows that because of course the first thing that anybody takes out of anybody's writing are the adjectives. You see of yourself how true it is that which I have just said.

Beside the nouns and the adjectives there are verbs and adverbs. Verbs and adverbs are more interesting. In the first place they have one very nice quality and that is that they can be so mistaken. It is wonderful the number of mistakes a verb can make and that is equally true of its adverb. Nouns and adjectives never can make mistakes can never be mistaken but verbs can be so endlessly, both as to what they do and how

211

they agree or disagree with whatever they do. The same is true of adverbs.

In that way any one can see that verbs and adverbs are more interesting than nouns and adjectives.

Beside being able to be mistaken and to make mistakes verbs can change to look like themselves or to look like something else, they are, so to speak on the move and adverbs move with them and each of them find themselves not at all annoying but very often very much mistaken. That is the reason any one can like what verbs can do. Then comes the thing that can of all things be most mistaken and they are prepositions. Prepositions can live one long life being really being nothing but absolutely nothing but mistaken and that makes them irritating if you feel that way about mistakes but certainly something that you can be continuously using and everlastingly enjoying. I like prepositions the best of all, and pretty soon we will go more completely into that.

Then there are articles. Articles are interesting just as nouns and adjectives are not. And why are they interesting just as nouns and adjectives are not. They are interesting because they do what a noun might do if a noun was not so unfortunately so completely unfortunately the name of something. Articles please, a and an and the please as the name that follows cannot please. They the names that is the nouns cannot please, because after all you know well after all that is what Shakespeare meant when he talked about a rose by any other name.

I hope now no one can have any illusion about a noun or about the adjective that goes with the noun.

But an article an article remains as a delicate and a varied something and any one who wants to write with articles and knows how to use them will always have the pleasure that using something that is varied and alive can give. That is what articles are.

Beside that there are conjunctions, and a conjunction is not varied but it has a force that need not make any one feel that they are dull. Conjunctions have made themselves live by their work. They work and as they work they live and even when they do not work and in these days they do not always live by work still nevertheless they do live.

So you see why I like to write with prepositions and conjunctions and articles and verbs and adverbs but not with nouns and adjectives. If you read my writing you will you do see what I mean.

Of course then there are pronouns. Pronouns are not as bad as nouns because in the first place practically they cannot have adjectives go with them. That already makes them better than nouns.

Then beside not being able to have adjectives go with them, they of course are not really the name of anything. They represent some one but they are not its or his name. In not being his or its or her name they already have a greater possibility of being something than if they were as a noun is the name of any-thing. Now actual given names of people are more lively than nouns which are the name of anything and I suppose that this is because after all the name is only given to that person when they are born, there is at least the element of choice even the element of change and anybody can be pretty well able to do what they like, they may be born Walter and become Hub, in such a way they are not like a noun. A noun has been the name of something for such a very long time.

That is the reason that slang exists it is to change the nouns which have been names for so long. I say again. Verbs and adverbs and articles and conjunc-tions and prepositions are lively because they all do something and as long as anything does something it keeps alive.

One might have in one's list added interjections but really interjections have nothing to do with anything not even with themselves. There so much for that. And now to go into the question of punctuation.

There are some punctuations that are interesting and there are some punctuations that are not. Let us begin with the punctuations that are not. Of these the one but the first and the most the completely most uninteresting is the question mark. The question mark is alright when it is all alone when it is used as a brand on cattle or when it could be used in decoration but connected with writing it is completely entirely com-pletely uninteresting. It is evident that if you ask a

214

question you ask a question but anybody who can read at all knows when a question is a question as it is written in writing. Therefore I ask you therefore wherefore should one use it the question mark. Beside it does not in its form go with ordinary printing and so it pleases neither the eye nor the ear and it is therefore like a noun, just an unnecessary name of something. A question is a question, anybody can know that a question is a question and so why add to it the question mark when it is already there when the question is already there in the writing. Therefore I never could bring myself to use a question mark, I always found it positively revolting, and now very few do use it. Exclamation marks have the same difficulty and also quotation marks, they are unnecessary, they are ugly, they spoil the line of the writing or the printing and anyway what is the use, if you do not know that a question is a question what is the use of its being a question. The same thing is true of an exclamation. And the same thing is true of a quotation. When I first began writing I found it simply impossible to use question marks and quotation marks and exclamation points and now anybody sees it that way. Perhaps some day they will see it some other way but now at any rate anybody can and does see it that way.

So there are the uninteresting things in punctuation uninteresting in a way that is perfectly obvious, and so we do not have to go any farther into that.

There are besides dashes and dots, and these might be interesting spaces might be interesting. They might if one felt that way about them.

One other little punctuation mark one can have feelings about and that is the apostrophe for possession. Well feel as you like about that, I can see and I do see that for many that for some the possessive case apostrophe has a gentle tender insinuation that makes it very difficult to definitely decide to do without it. One does do without it, I do, I mostly always do, but I cannot deny that from time to time I feel myself having regrets and from time to time I put it in to make the possessive case. I absolutely do not like it all alone when it is outside the word when the word is a plural, no then positively and definitely no, I do not like it and in leaving it out I feel no regret, there it is unnecessary and not ornamental but inside a word and its s well perhaps, perhaps it does appeal by its weakness to your weakness. At least at any rate from time to time I do find myself letting it alone if it has come in and sometimes it has come in. I cannot positively deny but that I do from time to time let it come in.

So now to come to the real question of punctuation, periods, commas, colons, semi-colons and capitals and small letters.

I have had a long and complicated life with all these.

Let us begin with these I use the least first and

these are colons and semi-colons, one might add to these commas.

When I first began writing, I felt that writing should go on, I still do feel that it should go on but when I first began writing I was completely possessed by the necessity that writing should go on and if writing should go on what had colons and semi-colons to do with it, what had commas to do with it, what had periods to do with it what had small letters and capitals to do with it to do with writing going on which was at that time the most profound need I had in connection with writing. What had colons and semi-colons to do with it what had commas to do with it what had periods to do with it.

What had periods to do with it. Inevitably no matter how completely I had to have writing go on, physically one had to again and again stop sometime and if one had to again and again stop some time then periods had to exist. Beside I had always liked the look of periods and I liked what they did. Stopping sometime did not really keep one from going on, it was nothing that interfered, it was only something that happened, and as it happened as a perfectly natural happening, I did believe in periods and I used them. I really never stopped using them.

Beside that periods might later come to have a life of their own to commence breaking up things in arbitrary ways, that has happened lately with me in a poem I have written called Winning His Way, later I

217

will read you a little of it. By the time I had written this poem about three years ago periods had come to have for me completely a life of their own. They could begin to act as they thought best and one might interrupt one's writing with them that is not really interrupt one's writing with them but one could come to stop arbitrarily stop at times in one's writing and so they could be used and you could use them. Periods could come to exist in this way and they could come in this way to have a life of their own. They did not serve you in any servile way as commas and colons and semi-colons do. Yes you do feel what I mean.

Periods have a life of their own a necessity of their own a feeling of their own a time of their own. And that feeling that life that necessity that time can express itself in an infinite variety that is the reason that I have always remained true to periods so much so that as I say recently I have felt that one could need them more than one had ever needed them.

You can see what an entirely different thing a period is from a comma, a colon or a semi-colon.

There are two different ways of thinking about colons and semi-colons you can think of them as commas and as such they are purely servile or you can think of them as periods and then using them can make you feel adventurous. I can see that one might feel about them as periods but I myself never have, I began unfortunately to feel them as a comma and commas are servile they have no life of their own they are dependent upon use and convenience and they are put there just for practical purposes. Semi-colons and colons had for me from the first completely this character the character that a comma has and not the character that a period has and therefore and definitely I have never used them. But now dimly and definitely I do see that they might well possibly they might have in them something of the character of the period and so it might have been an adventure to use them. I really do not think so. I think however lively they are or disguised they are they are definitely more comma than period and so really I cannot regret not having used them. They are more powerful more imposing more pretentious than a comma but they are a comma all the same. They really have within them deeply within them fundamentally within them the comma nature. And now what does a comma do and what has it to do and why do I feel as I do about them.

What does a comma do.

I have refused them so often and left them out so much and did without them so continually that I have come finally to be indifferent to them. I do not now care whether you put them in or not but for a long time I felt very definitely about them and would have nothing to do with them.

As I say commas are servile and they have no life of their own, and their use is not a use, it is a way of replacing one's own interest and I do decidedly like to like my own interest my own interest in what I am doing. A comma by helping you along holding your coat for you and putting on your shoes keeps you from living your life as actively as you should lead it and to me for many years and I still do feel that way about it only now I do not pay as much attention to them, the use of them was positively degrading. Let me tell you what I feel and what I mean and what I felt and what I meant.

When I was writing those long sentences of The Making of Americans, verbs active present verbs with long dependent adverbial clauses became a passion with me. I have told you that I recognize verbs and adverbs aided by prepositions and conjunctions with pronouns as possessing the whole of the active life of writing.

Complications make eventually for simplicity and therefore I have always liked dependent adverbial clauses. I have liked dependent adverbial clauses because of their variety of dependence and independence. You can see how loving the intensity of complication of these things that commas would be degrading. Why if you want the pleasure of concentrating on the final simplicity of excessive complication would you want any artificial aid to bring about that simplicity. Do you see now why I feel about the comma as I did and as I do.

Think about anything you really like to do and you will see what I mean.

When it gets really difficult you want to disentangle rather than to cut the knot, at least so anybody feels who is working with any thread, so anybody feels who is working with any tool so anybody feels who is writing any sentence or reading it after it has been written. And what does a comma do, a comma does nothing but make easy a thing that if you like it enough is easy enough without the comma. A long complicated sentence should force itself upon you, make you know yourself knowing it and the comma, well at the most a comma is a poor period that it lets you stop and take a breath but if you want to take a breath you ought to know yourself that you want to take a breath. It is not like stopping altogether which is what a period does stopping altogether has something to do with going on, but taking a breath well you are always taking a breath and why emphasize one breath rather than another breath. Anyway that is the way I felt about it and I felt that about it very very strongly. And so I almost never used a comma. The longer, the more complicated the sentence the greater the number of the same kinds of words I had following one after another, the more the very many more I had of them the more I felt the passionate need of their taking care of themselves by themselves and not helping them, and thereby enfeebling them by putting in a comma.

So that is the way I felt punctuation in prose, in poetry it is a little different but more so and later I will go into that. But that is the way I felt about punctuation in prose.

Another part of punctuation is capital letters and small letters. Anybody can really do as they please about that and in English printing one may say that they always have.

If you read older books you will see that they do pretty well what they please with capitals and small letters and I have always felt that one does do pretty well what one pleases with capitals and small letters. Sometimes one feels that Italians should be with a capital and sometimes with a small letter, one can feel like that about almost anything. I myself do not feel like that about proper names, I rather like to look at them with a capital on them but I can perfectly understand that a great many do not feel that way about it. In short in prose capitals and small letters have really nothing to do with the inner life of sentences and paragraphs as the other punctuation marks have as I have just been saying.

We still have capitals and small letters and probably for some time we will go on having them but actually the tendency is always toward diminishing capitals and quite rightly because the feeling that goes with them is less and less of a feeling and so slowly and inevitably just as with horses capitals will have gone away. They will come back from time to time but perhaps never really come back to stay.

Perhaps yes perhaps not but really and inevitably really it really does not really make any difference.

But and they will be with us as long as human beings continue to exist and have a vocabulary, sentences and paragraphs will be with us and therefore inevitably and really periods will be with us and it is of these things that will be always inevitably with us in prose and in poetry because prose and also poetry will also always always be with us that I will go on telling to you all I know.

Sentences and paragraphs. Sentences are not emotional but paragraphs are. I can say that as often as I like and it always remains as it is, something that is.

I said I found this out first in listening to Basket my dog drinking. And anybody listening to any dog's drinking will see what I mean.

When I wrote The Making of Americans I tried to break down this essential combination by making enormously long sentences that would be as long as the longest paragraph and so to see if there was really and truly this essential difference between paragraphs and sentences, if one went far enough with this thing with making the sentences long enough to be as long as any paragraph and so producing in them the balance of a paragraph not a balance of a sentence, because of course the balance of a paragraph is not the same balance as the balance of a sentence.

It is only necessary to read anything in order to

know that. I say if I succeeded in making my sentences so long that they held within themselves the balance of both both sentences and paragraphs, what was the result.

I did in some sentences in The Making of Americans succeed in doing this thing in creating a balance that was neither the balance of a sentence nor the balance of a paragraph and in doing so I felt dimly that I had done something that was not leading to anything because after all you should not lose two things in order to have one thing because in doing so you make writing just that much less varied.

That is one thing about what I did. There is also another thing and that was a very important thing, in doing this in achieving something that had neither the balance of a sentence nor the balance of a paragraph but a balance a new balance that had to do with a sense of movement of time included in a given space which as I have already said is a definitely American thing.

An American can fill up a space in having his movement of time by adding unexpectedly anything and yet getting within the included space everything he had intended getting.

A young french boy he is a red-haired descendant of the niece of Madame Recamier went to America for two weeks most unexpectedly and I said to him what did you notice most over there. Well he said at first they were not as different from us frenchmen as I expected them to be and then I did see that they were that they were different. And what, said I, well he said, when a train was going by at a terrific pace and we waved a hat the engine driver could make a bell quite carelessly go ting ting ting, the way anybody playing at a thing could do, it was not if you know what I mean professional he said. Perhaps you do see the connection with that and my sentences that had no longer the balance of sentences because they were not the parts of a paragraph nor were they a paragraph but they had made in so far as they had come to be so long and with the balance of their own that they had they had become something that was a whole thing and in so being they had a balance which was the balance of a space completely not filled but created by something moving as moving is not as moving should be. As I said Henry James in his later writing had had a dim feeling that this was what he knew he should do.

And so though as I say there must always be sentences and paragraphs the question can really be asked must there always be sentences and paragraphs is it not possible to achieve in itself and not by sentences and paragraphs the combination that sentences are not emotional and paragraphs are.

In a book called How to Write I worked a lot at this thing trying to find out just exactly what the balance the unemotional balance of a sentence is and what the emotional balance of a paragraph is and if it were possible to make even in a short sentence the two things come to be one. I think I did a few times succeed. Will you listen to one or two sentences where I did think I had done this thing.

He looks like a young man grown old.
HOW TO WRITE. (PLAIN EDITION) RANDOM HOUSE. PAGE 25.

It looks like a garden but he had hurt himself by accident.
HOW TO WRITE. PAGE 26.

A dog which you have never had before has sighed.
HOW TO WRITE. PAGE 27.

Once when they were nearly ready they had ordered it to close.
HOW TO WRITE. PAGE 29.

If a sound is made which grows louder and then stops how many times may it be repeated.
HOW TO WRITE. PAGE 89.

Battles are named because there have been hills which have made a hill in a battle.
HOW TO WRITE. PAGE 89.

A bay and hills hills are surrounded by their having their distance very near.
HOW TO WRITE. PAGE 89.

226

Poplars indeed will be and may be indeed will be cut down and will be sawn up and indeed will be used as wood and may be used for wood.

HOW TO WRITE. PAGE 90.

The thing to remember is that if it is not if it is not what having left it to them makes it be very likely as likely as they would be after all after all choosing choosing to be here on time.

HOW TO WRITE. PAGE 259.

In spite of my intending to write about grammar and poetry I am still writing about grammar and prose, but and of course it may or may not be true if you find out essentially what prose is and essentially what poetry is may you not have an exciting thing happening as I had it happen with sentences and paragraphs.

After all the natural way to count is not that one and one make two but to go on counting by one and one as chinamen do as anybody does as Spaniards do as my little aunts did. One and one and one and one and one. That is the natural way to go on counting.

Now what has this to do with poetry. It has a lot to do with poetry.

Everything has a lot to do with poetry everything has a lot to do with prose.

And has prose anything to do with poetry and has poetry anything to do with prose.

And what have nouns to do with poetry and periods

and capital letters. The other punctuation marks we never have to mention again. People may do as they like with them but we never have to mention them. But nouns still have to be mentioned because in coming to avoid nouns a great deal happens and has happened. It was one of the things that happened in a book I called Tender Buttons.

In The Making of Americans a long a very long prose book made up of sentences and paragraphs and the new thing that was something neither the sentence or the paragraph each one alone or in combination had ever done, I said I had gotten rid of nouns and adjectives as much as possible by the method of living in adverbs in verbs in pronouns, in adverbial clauses written or implied and in conjunctions.

But and after I had gone as far as I could in these long sentences and paragraphs that had come to do something else I then began very short things and in doing very short things I resolutely realized nouns and decided not to get around them but to meet them, to handle in short to refuse them by using them and in that way my real acquaintance with poetry was begun.

I will try to tell a little more clearly and in more detail just what happened and why it was if it was like natural counting, that is counting by one one one one one.

Nouns as you all know are the names of anything and as the names of anything of course one has had to use them. And what have they done. And what has any one done with them. That is something to know. It is as you may say as I may say a great deal to know.

Nouns are the name of anything and anything is named, that is what Adam and Eve did and if you like it is what anybody does, but do they go on just using the name until perhaps they do not know what the name is or if they do know what the name is they do not care about what the name is. This may happen of course it may. And what has poetry got to do with this and what has prose and if everything like a noun which is a name of anything is to be avoided what takes place. And what has that to do with poetry. A great deal I think and all this too has to do with other things with short and long lines and rhymes.

But first what is poetry and what is prose. I wonder if I can tell you.

We do know a little now what prose is. Prose is the balance the emotional balance that makes the reality of paragraphs and the unemotional balance that makes the reality of sentences and having realized completely realized that sentences are not emotional while paragraphs are, prose can be the essential balance that is made inside something that combines the sentence and the paragraph, examples of this I have been reading to you.

Now if that is what prose is and that undoubtedly

is what prose is you can see that prose real prose really great written prose is bound to be made up more of verbs adverbs prepositions prepositional clauses and conjunctions than nouns. The vocabulary in prose of course is important if you like vocabulary is always important, in fact one of the things that you can find out and that I experimented with a great deal in How to Write vocabulary in itself and by itself can be interesting and can make sense. Anybody can know that by thinking of words. It is extraordinary how it is impossible that a vocabulary does not make sense. But that is natural indeed inevitable because a vocabulary is that by definition, and so because this is so the vocabulary in respect to prose is less important than the parts of speech, and the internal balance and the movement within a given space.

So then we understand we do know what prose is.

But what is poetry.

Is it more or is it less difficult to know what poetry is. I have sometimes thought it more difficult to know what poetry is but now that I do know what poetry is and if I do know what poetry is then it is not more difficult to know what it is than to know what prose is.

What is poetry.

Poetry has to do with vocabulary just as prose has not.

So you see prose and poetry are not at all alike. They are completely different.

Poetry is I say essentially a vocabulary just as prose is essentially not.

And what is the vocabulary of which poetry absolutely is. It is a vocabulary entirely based on the noun as prose is essentially and determinately and vigorously not based on the noun.

Poetry is concerned with using with abusing, with losing with wanting, with denying with avoiding with adoring with replacing the noun. It is doing that always doing that, doing that and doing nothing but that. Poetry is doing nothing but using losing refusing and pleasing and betraying and caressing nouns. That is what poetry does, that is what poetry has to do no matter what kind of poetry it is. And there are a great many kinds of poetry.

When I said.

A rose is a rose is a rose is a rose.

And then later made that into a ring I made poetry and what did I do I caressed completely caressed and addressed a noun.

Now let us think of poetry any poetry all poetry and let us see if this is not so. Of course it is so anybody can know that.

I have said that a noun is a name of anything by definition that is what it is and a name of anything is not interesting because once you know its name the enjoyment of naming it is over and therefore in writing prose names that is nouns are completely uninteresting. But and that is a thing to be remembered you can love a name and if you love a name then saying that name any number of times only makes you love it more, more violently more persistently more tormentedly. Anybody knows how anybody calls out the name of anybody one loves. And so that is poetry really loving the name of anything and that is not prose. Yes any of you can know that.

Poetry like prose has lived through a good deal. Anybody or anything lives through a good deal. Sometimes it included everything and sometimes it includes only itself and there can be any amount of less and more at any time of its existence.

Of course when poetry really began it practically included everything it included narrative and feelings and excitements and nouns so many nouns and all emotions. It included narrative but now it does not include narrative.

I often wonder how I am ever to come to know all that I am to know about narrative. Narrative is a problem to me. I worry about it a good deal these days and I will not write or lecture about it yet, because I am still too worried about it worried about knowing what it is and how it is and where it is and how it is and how it will be what it is. However as I say now and at this time I do not I will not go into that. Suffice it to say that for the purpose of poetry it has now for a long time not had anything to do with being there.

Perhaps it is a mistake perhaps not that it is no longer there.

I myself think that something else is going to happen about narrative and I work at it a great deal at this time not work but bother about it. Bother is perhaps the better word for what I am doing just now about narrative. But anyway to go back to poetry.

Poetry did then in beginning include everything and it was natural that it should because then everything including what was happening could be made real to anyone by just naming what was happening in other words by doing what poetry always must do by living in nouns.

Nouns are the name of anything. Think of all that early poetry, think of Homer, think of Chaucer, think of the Bible and you will see what I mean you will really realize that they were drunk with nouns, to name to know how to name earth sea and sky and all that was in them was enough to make them live and love in names, and that is what poetry is it is a state of knowing and feeling a name. I know that now but I have only come to that knowledge by long writing.

So then as I say that is what poetry was and slowly as everybody knew the names of everything poetry had less and less to do with everything. Poetry did not change, poetry never changed, from the beginning until now and always in the future poetry will concern itself with the names of things. The names may be repeated in different ways and very soon I will go into that matter but now and always poetry is created by naming names the names of something the names of somebody the names of anything. Nouns are the names of things and so nouns are the basis of poetry.

Before we go any further there is another matter. Why are the lines of poetry short, so much shorter than prose, why do they rhyme, why in order to complete themselves do they have to end with what they began, why are all these things the things that are in the essence of poetry even when the poetry was long even when now the poetry has changed its form.

Once more the answer is the same and that is that such a way to express oneself is the natural way when one expresses oneself in loving the name of anything. Think what you do when you do do that when you love the name of anything really love its name. Inevitably you express yourself in that way, in the way poetry expresses itself that is in short lines in repeating what you began in order to do it again. Think of how you talk to anything whose name is new to you a lover a baby or a dog or a new land or any part of it. Do you not inevitably repeat what you call out and is that calling out not of necessity in short lines. Think about it and you will see what I mean by what you feel.

So as I say poetry is essentially the discovery, the love, the passion for the name of anything.

Now to come back to how I know what I know about poetry.

I was writing The Making of Americans, I was completely obsessed by the inner life of everything including generations of everybody's living and I was writing prose, prose that had to do with the balancing the inner balancing of everything. I have already told you all about that.

And then, something happened and I began to discover the names of things, that is not discover the names but discover the things the things to see the things to look at and in so doing I had of course to name them not to give them new names but to see that I could find out how to know that they were there by their names or by replacing their names. And how was I to do so. They had their names and naturally I called them by the names they had and in doing so having begun looking at them I called them by their names with passion and that made poetry, I did not mean it to make poetry but it did, it made the Tender Buttons, and the Tender Buttons was very good poetry it made a lot more poetry, and I will now more and more tell about that and how it happened.

I discovered everything then and its name, discovered it and its name. I had always known it and its name but all the same I did discover it.

I remember very well when I was a little girl and I and my brother found as children will the love poems of their very very much older brother. This older brother had just written one and it said that he had often sat and looked at any little square of grass and it had been just a square of grass as grass is, but now he was in love and so the little square of grass was all filled with birds and bees and butterflies, the difference was what love was. The poem was funny we and he knew the poem was funny but he was right, being in love made him make poetry, and poetry made him feel the things and their names, and so I repeat nouns are poetry.

So then in Tender Buttons I was making poetry but and it seriously troubled me, dimly I knew that nouns made poetry but in prose I no longer needed the help of nouns and in poetry did I need the help of nouns. Was there not a way of naming things that would not invent names, but mean names without naming them.

I had always been very impressed from the time that I was very young by having had it told me and then afterwards feeling it myself that Shakespeare in the forest of Arden had created a forest without mentioning the things that make a forest. You feel it all but he does not name its names.

Now that was a thing that I too felt in me the need of making it be a thing that could be named without using its name. After all one had known its name anything's name for so long, and so the name was not new but the thing being alive was always new.

What was there to do.

I commenced trying to do something in Tender Buttons about this thing. I went on and on trying to do this thing. I remember in writing An Acquaintance With Description looking at anything until something that was not the name of that thing but was in a way that actual thing would come to be written.

Naturally, and one may say that is what made Walt Whitman naturally that made the change in the form of poetry, that we who had known the names so long did not get a thrill from just knowing them. We that is any human being living has inevitably to feel the thing anything being existing, but the name of that thing of that anything is no longer anything to thrill any one except children. So as everybody has to be a poet, what was there to do. This that I have just described, the creating it without naming it, was what broke the rigid form of the noun the simple noun poetry which now was broken.

Of course you all do know that when I speak of naming anything, I include emotions as well as things.

So then there we were and what were we to do about it. Go on, of course go on what else does anybody do, so I did, I went on.

Of course you might say why not invent new names new languages but that cannot be done. It takes a

237

tremendous amount of inner necessity to invent even one word, one can invent imitating movements and emotions in sounds, and in the poetical language of some languages you have that, the german language as a language suffers from this what the words mean sound too much like what they do, and children do these things by one sort or another of invention but this has really nothing to do with language. Language as a real thing is not imitation either of sounds or colors or emotions it is an intellectual recreation and there is no possible doubt about it and it is going to go on being that as long as humanity is anything. So every one must stay with the language their language that has come to be spoken and written and which has in it all the history of its intellectual recreation.

And so for me the problem of poetry was and it began with Tender Buttons to constantly realize the thing anything so that I could recreate that thing. I struggled I struggled desperately with the recreation and the avoidance of nouns as nouns and yet poetry being poetry nouns are nouns. Let me read you bits of the Portrait of Sherwood Anderson and The Birthplace of Bonnes to show you what I mean.

Can anybody tell by looking which was the towel used for cooking.

PORTRAITS AND PRAYERS. PAGE 162.

A VERY VALENTINE

Very fine is my valentine.

Very fine and very mine.

Very mine is my valentine very mine and
very fine.

Very fine is my valentine and mine, very fine
very mine and mine is my valentine.

PORTRAITS AND PRAYERS. PAGE 152.

BUNDLES FOR THEM

A HISTORY OF GIVING BUNDLES

We were able to notice that each one in a way
carried a bundle, they were not a trouble to them
nor were they all bundles as some of them were
chickens some of them pheasants some of them
sheep and some of them bundles, they were not
a trouble to them and then indeed we learned
that it was the principal recreation and they
were so arranged that they were not given away,
and today they were given away.

I will not look at them again.

They will not look for them again.

They have not seen them here again.

They are in there and we hear them again.

In which way are stars brighter than they
are. When we have come to this decision. We
mention many thousands of buds. And when I
close my eyes I see them.

If you hear her snore

It is not before you love her

You love her so that to be her beau is very
lovely

She is sweetly there and her curly hair is very
lovely.

She is sweetly here and I am very near and
that is very lovely.

She is my tender sweet and her little feet are
stretched out well which is a treat and very
lovely.

Her little tender nose is between her little eyes
which close and are very lovely.

She is very lovely and mine which is very
lovely.

PORTRAITS AND PRAYERS. PAGE 154.

I found in longer things like Operas and Plays and
Portraits and Lucy Church Amiably and An Acquaintance With Description that I could come nearer
to avoiding names in recreating something.

That brings us to the question will poetry continue
to be necessarily short as it has been as really good
poetry has been for a very long time. Perhaps not
and why not.

If enough is new to you to name or not name, and
these two things come to the same thing, can you go
on long enough. Yes I think so.

So then poetry up to the present time has been a

poetry of nouns a poetry of naming something of really naming that thing passionately completely passionately naming that thing by its name.

Slowly and particularly during the nineteenth century the English nineteenth century everybody had come to know too well very much too well the name anything had when you called it by its name.

That is something that inevitably happened. And what else could they do. They had to go on doing what they did, that is calling anything by its name passionately but if as I say they really knew its name too well could they call it its name simply in that way. Slowly they could not.

And then Walt Whitman came. He wanted really wanted to express the thing and not call it by its name. He worked very hard at that, and he called it Leaves of Grass because he wanted it to be as little a well known name to be called upon passionately as possible. I do not at all know whether Whitman knew that he wanted to do this but there is no doubt at all but that is what he did want to do.

You have the complete other end of this thing in a poet like Longfellow, I cite him because a commonplace poet shows you more readily and clearly just what the basis of poetry is than a better one. And Longfellow knew all about calling out names, he on the whole did it without passion but he did it very well.

Of course in the history of poetry there have been

many who have also tried to name the thing without naming its names, but this is not a history of poets it is a telling what I know about poetry.

And so knowing all this about poetry I struggled more and more with this thing. I say I knew all this about poetry but I did not really know all this then about poetry, I was coming to know then then when I was writing commencing to know what I do now know about prose but I did not then know anything really to know it of what I now know about poetry.

And so in Tender Buttons and then on and on I struggled with the ridding myself of nouns, I knew nouns must go in poetry as they had gone in prose if anything that is everything was to go on meaning something.

And so I went on with this exceeding struggle of knowing really knowing what a thing was really knowing it knowing anything I was seeing anything I was feeling so that its name could be something, by its name coming to be a thing in itself as it was but would not be anything just and only as a name.

I wonder if you do see what I mean.

What I mean by what I have just said is this. I had to feel anything and everything that for me was existing so intensely that I could put it down in writing as a thing in itself without at all necessarily using its name. The name of a thing might be something in itself if it could come to be real enough but just as a name it was not enough something. At any rate that is the way I felt and still do feel about it.

And so I went through a very long struggle and in this struggle I began to be troubled about narrative a narrative of anything that was or might be happening.

The newspapers tell us about it but they tell it to us as nouns tell it to us that is they name it, and in naming it, it as a telling of it is no longer anything. That is what a newspaper is by definition just as a noun is a name by definition.

And so I was slowly beginning to know something about what poetry was. And here was the question if in poetry one could lose the noun as I had really and truly lost it in prose would there be any difference between poetry and prose. As this thing came once more to be a doubt inside me I began to work very hard at poetry.

At that time I wrote Before the Flowers of Friendship Faded Friendship Faded and there I went back again to a more or less regular form to see whether inside that regular form I could do what I was sure needed to be done and also to find out if eventually prose and poetry were one or not one.

In writing this poem I found I could be very gay I could be very lively in poetry, I could use very few nouns in poetry and call out practically no names in poetry and yet make poetry really feel and sound as poetry, but was it what I wanted that should be done.

But it did not decide anything for me but it did help me in my way.

XII

I am very hungry when I drink,
I need to leave it when I have it held,

They will be white with which they know they see, that darker makes it be a color white for me, white is not shown when I am dark indeed with red despair who comes who has to care that they will let me a little lie like now I like to lie I like to live I like to die I like to lie and live and die and live and die and by and by I like to live and die and by and by they need to sew, the difference is that sewing makes it bleed and such with them in all the way of seed and seeding and repine and they will which is mine and not all mine who can be thought curious of this of all of that made it and come lead it and done weigh it and mourn and sit upon it know it for ripeness without deserting all of it of which without which it has not been born. Oh no not to be thirsty with the thirst of hunger not alone to know that they plainly and ate or wishes. Any little one will kill himself for milk.

BEFORE THE FLOWERS OF FRIENDSHIP FADED
FRIENDSHIP FADED (PLAIN EDITION). PAGE 14.

XIV

It could be seen very nicely
That doves have each a heart,
Each one is always seeing that they could not
    be apart,
A little lake makes fountains
And fountains have no flow,
And a dove has need of flying
And water can be low,
Let me go.
Any week is what they seek
When they have to halve a beak.
I like a painting on a wall of doves
And what do they do,
They have hearts
They are apart
Little doves are winsome
But not when they are little and left.

BEFORE THE FLOWERS OF FRIENDSHIP FADED
FRIENDSHIP FADED (PLAIN EDITION). PAGE 16.

I decided and Lucy Church Amiably had been an
attempt to do it, I decided that if one definitely completely replaced the noun by the thing in itself, it
was eventually to be poetry and not prose which
would have to deal with everything that was not
movement in space. There could no longer be form
to decide anything, narrative that is not newspaper
narrative but real narrative must of necessity be told

by any one having come to the realization that the noun must be replaced not by inner balance but by the thing in itself and that will eventually lead to everything. I am working at this thing and what will it do this I do not know but I hope that I will know. In the Four In America I have gone on beginning but I am sure that there is in this what there is that it is necessary to do if one is to do anything or everything. Do you see what I mean. Well anyway that is the way that I do now feel about it, and this is all that I do know, and I do believe in knowing all I do know, about prose and poetry. The rest will come considerably later.

GERTRUDE STEIN was born in Pennsylvania in 1874. At Radcliffe she was an outstanding student of William James in psychology, and conducted laboratory experiments with Hugo Munsterberg, which led her to study the anatomy of the brain at Johns Hopkins. In 1902 she joined her brother Leo in Paris, and lived abroad until her death in 1946. Her salon in the rue de Fleurus, over which she presided with Alice B. Toklas, became the gathering place of prominent writers and painters, among them Sherwood Anderson and Hemingway, Matisse and Picasso.

VINTAGE CRITICISM,
LITERATURE, MUSIC, AND ART

VINTAGE BELLES–LETTRES